You Might Need A Jacket
Hilarious Stories of Wacky Sports Parents

BY EARL AUSTIN, JR.

P.O. Box 2535
Florissant, Mo 63033

Copyright ©2009 by Earl Austin, Jr.

All Rights reserved. No part of this book may be reproduced or transmitted in any forms by any means, electronic, mechanical, photocopy, recording or otherwise, without the consent of the Publisher, except as provided by USA copyright law.

Edited by: Editor Jill Ronsely
Writer & Editor: Earl Austin Jr.
Front & Back Cover Design: Angelita Jackson
Cover Design ©2009 Angelita Jackson

Manufactured in the United States of America

Library of Congress Control Number: 2009906871
ISBN 13: 9780981991313

You can purchase additional copies of this publication by going online at www.prioritybooks.com and www.earlaustinjr.com. If you have any comments or additional straitjacket stories to tell, you can contact Earl Austin Jr. at eaustin@stlamerican.com.

For information regarding discounts for bulk purchases, please contact Prioritybooks Publications at www.prioritybooks.com or info@prioritybooks.com.

Published by Prioritybooks Publications
Missouri

Dedication

This book is dedicated to all the parents.

Acknowledgements

I would like to thank some special people who have played a big role in making this publication possible. The front and back covers were designed by Angelita Jackson, who is one of the most talented graphic artists in the business today. I would also like to thank my new publisher, Rose Beavers of Prioritybooks, for her support in my new endeavors. Many thanks to Frank Cusumano of KSDK-TV for writing the foreword to this book, as well as to my friends, Lou Potsou and Ronald Golden, for coming up with the term "straitjacket parent." To all the coaches, referees, kids and parents, I want to thank you for the stories you have shared with me in helping me put this book together.

I give special thanks to my new wife, Mrs. Judy Austin, for her unwavering love and support in everything I do. I love you, doll.

Finally, I want to thank my parents, Sandra and Earl Austin Sr., for the love and support they have given me my entire life. Mom, although you are no longer with us, your spirit is always present to help guide me. I miss you very much, but I know that you are in a better place and are watching over me, Courtney and Richard, and your grandsons.

Introduction

Hello, Sports Fans!

I would like to thank all of you for picking up a copy of my new book, You Might Need a Jacket: Hilarious Stories of Wacky Sports Parents. Over the past two decades, I have had the pleasure of covering the exploits of some of the most talented athletes ever to play in the St. Louis Metropolitan area. In that same time span, I have had the opportunity to meet many of the parents of these youngsters.

In most cases, when you have a successful young athlete, there is a caring and loving parent who has provided nurturing and support, and who has gone through great sacrifice to make sure his precious child receives everything he or she needs to succeed. Sometimes these parents go to great lengths, even taking extraordinary measures to make sure their children shine in the spotlight. In show business, the common term for such an individual is the stage parent. I have had a chance to witness many of the actions of these people during my time covering sports in St. Louis. This, in turn, led to the creation of a new term for sports parents: We call these people straitjacket parents. I don't think that needs any more explanation.

I must give credit to my friends Lou Potsou, who has been a mover and shaker in St. Louis' youth sports for decades, and basketball coach Ronald Golden, who came up with the phrase that accurately describes our sometimes overzealous mothers and fathers. These good folks mean well, and they truly love their children. However, the way they go about showing their love and support of their children's athletic endeavors can get them into some embarrassing situations—as well as into this book.

Some of the most mild-mannered and kind people I know can turn into raving lunatics when it comes to following their children's progress. The transformation can be quite eye-opening. As a rule, when I attend games, I rarely sit next to parents while their children are playing. I learned this lesson early in my career: Stay away from Mom and Dad while the game is going on! They can get a little wound up, as you might expect. When a parent comes to sit next to me, I have been known to move away or ask the parent to move to another seat.

Although this book centers on the parents and relatives of athletes from St. Louis, these people are hardly alone in their straitjacket behavior. It is an illness that runs rampant all around the world, from the youth sports fields all the way up to the big-time college and professional venues. Nobody is immune from this disease. If you have a kid who participates in youth sports, you are a prime candidate to be a straitjacket parent.

We've seen stories about these parents make national headlines, such as the eleven-year-old wrestler's father who lost his mind and attacked his son's opponent in the middle of the match when it became apparent that his son was about to be defeated. The father ran across the mat, picked up the little boy and threw him. Then he started walking toward the camera, pointing and screaming as if he were pro-wrestler Stone Cold Steve Austin. And what about the tragic case in Massachusetts several years ago, when two fathers got into a fight at a youth hockey game and one of them ended up killing the other?

In 2006, another hockey dad in Toronto was convicted of strangling a coach for not playing his eight-year-old son. Or how about the disturbing story, told on HBO's "Real Sports," about how parents had their eleven and twelve-year-old Little League Baseball-playing sons undergo

"Tommy John Surgery" to have the ligaments in their arms tightened, in order to help their futures as pitchers? Then there's the story of a youth football game in El Paso, Texas, in 2001, when one parent stabbed another in the head with a yard marker in front of a bunch of eight and nine-year-old players. Who can forget how a few years back, a youth football parent in Stockton, California, became an instant straitjacket legend when he ran across the field and delivered a bone-crushing blow to a child after he saw the kid deliver a late hit on his son, touching off a wild, parents-only brawl? And how about the father in France who was so obsessed with wanting his teenage children to succeed in tennis that he spiked the drinks of his children's opponents with an anti-depressant drug? His actions led to the death of one of those competitors, who fell asleep at the wheel of his car later that night. Yes, folks, it can get that serious.

One of the most famous straitjacket parents of all has to be the mother from Texas who was so enraged that her daughter did not make the high school cheerleading team that she tried to hire a hit man to have the mother of her daughter's cheerleading rival killed. She hoped this would make the successful girl so distraught that she would quit the squad, opening up a spot for her daughter. Wherever in the world you live, I'll bet you, too, have an interesting story to tell. If you ever go on YouTube, you can see some startling footage of straitjacket-parent behavior caught on tape. The more such stories I read, the more my jaw drops. Folks are serious about their children.

The parents of well-known professional athletes such as Venus and Serena Williams, Mary Pierce, LeBron James, Jelena Dokic, Eric Lindros, Vince Carter, Todd Marinovich and many others have made headlines of their own for straitjacket behavior. The list is endless. The stories are mostly humorous, and sometimes quite shocking. There was even a movie made in 1957, entitled Fear Strikes Out, based on the life story of former Major League Baseball player Jimmy Piersall (portrayed by Anthony Perkins), who was driven to a nervous breakdown by an overbearing straitjacket father (played by Karl Malden). Even celebrities such as former Major League Baseball star pitcher Roger Clemens and CNN talk-show host Larry King have been kicked out of their son's Little League baseball games.

Parents just want to see their children achieve the highest possible level of success. They dream of seeing their little ones become the next LeBron James, Tiger Woods, Shawn Johnson, Michael Phelps, Serena Williams or Tom Brady, and they will do almost anything to make that dream a reality. Some of these parents are former athletes who want to see their children carry on the family legacy. Some will spend incredible amounts of money to support their child's athletic pursuits. Others may never have played any sports, or may not have been very successful on the athletic field, so they try to live through the success of their children. And then there are those who simply have dollar signs in their eyes; they see their kids as the ticket to fame and fortune.

For years, I've written about young athletes and have enjoyed them immensely. However, this book is dedicated to those delightful parents who never cease to amaze me with what they will do in support of their children. This book is for them, and I want to have a little fun with good ol' Mom and Dad. But you don't necessarily have to be a parent to earn a spot in this book. We have stories of siblings, aunts, uncles and other family members who have gotten caught up in the madness. There's even the wife of a former All-Pro National Football League quarterback, who felt the need to call a local sports talk show and challenge comments made by her husband's head coach on live radio. As I said before, everyone is a candidate.

YOU MIGHT NEED A JACKET

Through my twenty-two years covering high school and youth sports, I have been able to collect nearly two hundred stories for this book, which is just a small sample of what goes on. Everyone has a story to tell about some wacky parent who just lost control at some point. Most of the stories in this book are humorous; however, some parents have been known to get a little too out of control. That is when things get serious, and none of us like to see that. Some of the events mentioned here may not be believed, but they actually happened in the St. Louis area. I chronicled many of these events in my column in the St. Louis American newspaper in 2004 and 2006. In this book, I get to discuss the events in more detail and add a few more logs to the fire.

For the most part, I have chosen not to reveal the identity of the straitjacket parent in order to protect the guilty. However, I know many of you will have fun trying to figure out the identity of each person as you read the stories. The names that are mentioned are the names of those who have given me their blessing and permission to identify them, brave souls that they are. Many of the parents mentioned in the book are people I know personally, and many are friends. Others are professional colleagues of mine in the sports media, including local television sports celebrity Frank Cusumano, of KSDK, who has written the foreword. To make sure I did not discriminate, I have mentioned some of my own family members and even myself, since at one time I exhibited some straitjacket behavior that I am not proud of. I guess I'm trying to say that in this book, nobody is safe.

I have witnessed many of these scenarios with my own eyes. Other stories have come from coaches and other observers of youth sports over the years, including parents who had no problem telling on each other. Another interesting source of material was the athletes themselves. That's right, Mom and Dad—some of your own children dropped a dime on you!

I hope everyone enjoys this humorous look at our parents. We love them all. We kid about their antics because we care. And remember, if you think you recognize yourself in some of the following stories, then you just might need a straitjacket of your own.

Thanks!
Have fun and enjoy the book.
Earl

Foreword

By Frank Cusumano

I can remember the moment like it was yesterday. It was eleven years ago. Alex, my oldest child, was five years old. He had just joined his first basketball team. He came out of the locker room in full uniform, all powder blue and polyester, with the proudest expression I had seen in his entire five years. He was going to be a basketball player, just like his dad had been, and he was feeling good.

I don't cry very often, but that day I did, for ten seconds. This was my son. This was my flesh and blood. My little buddy was going to be a player. I looked at him and saw myself twenty-five years earlier. My wife, the lovely Monique, looked over and said, "Are you crying?" I had to turn away. She told me to man up. She just didn't understand the romance I have always had with basketball. And when, for the first time, it was basketball with my son—well, it got to me.

My good friend, Earl Austin Jr., has written a book about how straitjacket parents carry on at their kids' sporting events. People who go above and beyond the call of duty for their children are chronicled in this book. It is an awesome read. Earl has seen it all. No one has watched more basketball games than Earl. No one has seen more crazy parents than Earl. And I don't know if anybody knows more about youth sports than Earl.

I have handled my obsession, my addiction to sports, by doing the following at my son's high school games: I usually sit in the top row, alone, often with a Bible, never saying a word out loud. Every once in a while, Monique will sit next to me. If I blurt out something, she will look at me and say, "If you say one more word, I am leaving." My response is usually, "Go!" But it took me a lot of time to get to this stage.

I loved sports so much. I want my two kids to work hard and try to be the best they can. But one day, I did something really stupid. When Alex was nine years old, he was pitching in a baseball game at Kirkwood. A line drive came screaming back at him, and he got hit square in the eye. A blood vessel in his eye broke. The blood came flowing out like he'd been shot with a gun. We rushed him to St. John's Hospital. His little sister, Brooke, got there later. She took one look at Alex, started crying and asked if he was going to die. The doctor said Alex was about a half-inch away from losing the eye. He needed thirty-five stitches.

The next day, I was off from work. Alex was feeling a little better. His team was playing a game at three p.m., and Monique wouldn't be home until seven. I casually mentioned to Alex that his team was going to have a game in a few hours.

Alex said, "Why are you telling me that?"

I said, "Mom is at work."

Alex said, "You would let me play?"

I said, "As long as you don't tell Mom and you play nothing but the outfield."

I took Alex to play in the game, where he went one for two with a walk. His mother never found out, and she won't find out unless she reads this book. I hope everybody in St. Louis—everybody who doesn't know Monique—reads this book.

 (Frank Cusumano is an award-winning television broadcaster for KSDK, the NBC affiliate in St. Louis. He is also the host of his own morning drive-time radio talk show on KFNS, entitled "The Press Box." Frank has been heavily involved in youth sports for several years as a coach.)

Strait Jacket Parents

What is a straitjacket parent? It's a staple, a universal theme. It's a parent who believes that his or her child can do no wrong. Straitjacket parents view life through rose-colored lenses, as far as their children are concerned. For instance, they believe that there's nothing wrong with their baby; it's everyone else who has the problem. When the child is out there on the playing field, the straitjacket parent sees nobody else but their little one. A straitjacket parent tends to have goals above ability for his or her child. When those goals are not achieved, it becomes easy to blame everyone else instead of looking in the mirror at the person who set these outlandish goals in the first place. .Finally, being a straitjacket parent means that you are a great enabler for your child. After all, it's all about them.

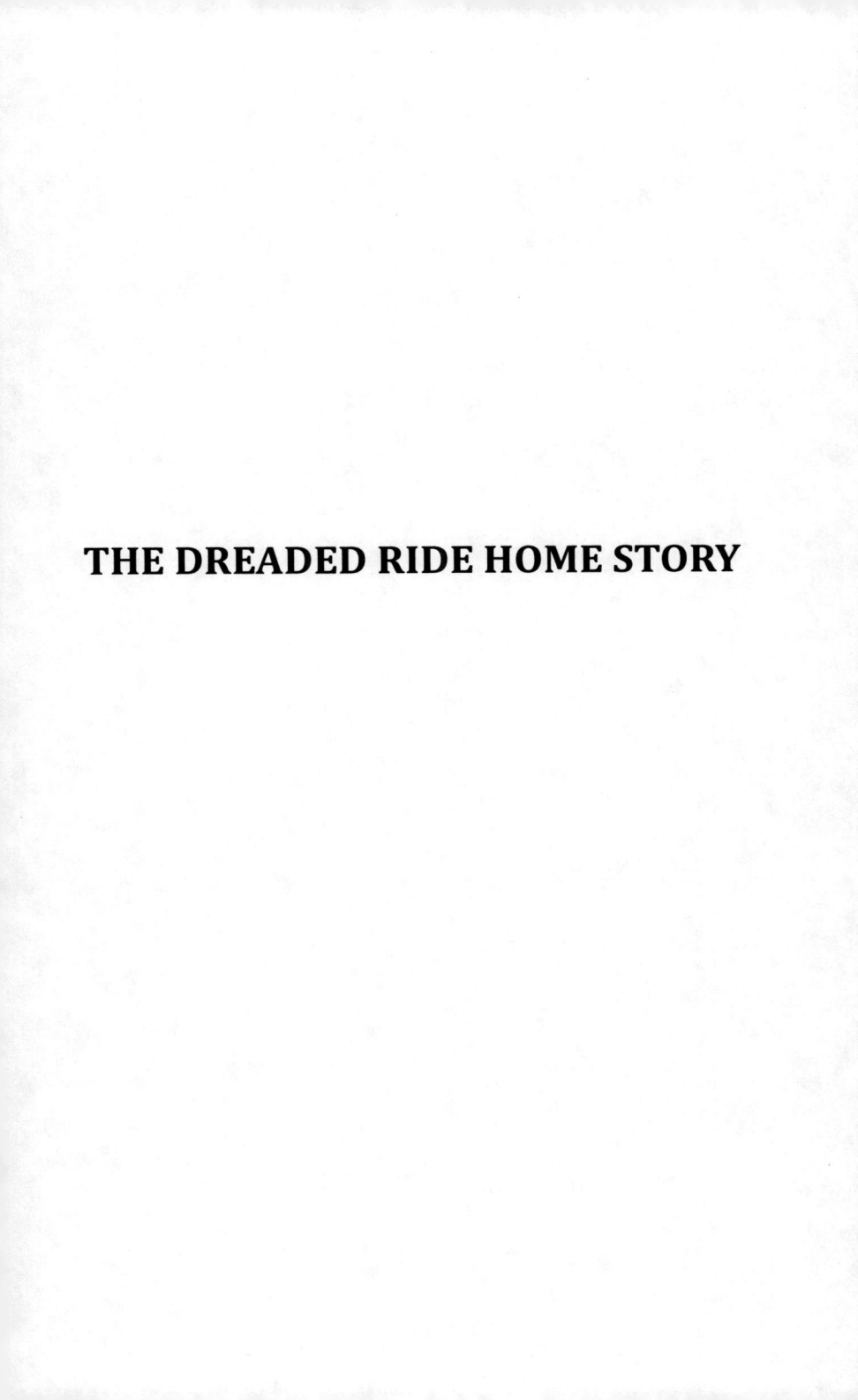

THE DREADED RIDE HOME STORY

The Dreaded Ride Home

If you have been a participant in youth sports or the parent of a youth athlete, you have experienced the "Dreaded Ride Home." There are no exceptions to this rule of youth sports. Everyone has been a part of the "Dreaded Ride Home" whether you were coming home from a sporting event, beauty pageant, spelling bee, science fair, music recital, the ballet or any other kind of activity. It is an unavoidable part of the growing up experience and this scene is played out every night in some automobile or passenger van around the world. All of us have been there and have taken the ride. That is why this is such a fitting opening chapter to this book. Everyone can relate to this one.

Just remember back to your youth sports days. It was a tough and emotional game and your team came up on the losing end and nobody is happy about it. Or your team may have won and your performance was not up to par in the eyes of your parents. However, there is still one more scene left to be played out in this drama. That, of course, is the "Dreaded Ride Home."

For parents, this is the perfect opportunity to critique and pick apart their children's performance during the game, on the way home. After spending the entire game being powerless, due to the distance of the bleachers in relation to the playing field, they now have their kids in close quarters with all of their post-game comments and ammunition gathered and ready. It is time to pounce. This is their chance to take out their frustrations from the game on somebody, who happens to be their kid.

I have witnessed one mother who would actually get herself psyched up for the ride home as if she were going to play a game herself. "I can't wait to get that boy in the car for the ride home," she would say. Another parent would take notes during the game and when it came time to drive home, he would unleash his laundry list of mistakes on his kid.

As you might expect, most kids hate the dreaded ride home. They are already feeling down in the dumps after losing a tough game and the chances are good that they have already gotten an earful from an unhappy losing coach in the locker room after the loss. The last thing they want to hear at that time is another lecture from another adult, especially a parent. But that doesn't stop Mom or Dad from moving in for the verbal smack-down. Not only does the kid have to hear about how poorly they played, but they also have to be subjected to the same old blather about how terrible the coach is and how the kid's teammates just don't measure up to their own kid's ability. If there was a kid on the other team that was a great player, you have to hear about how you don't measure up to that kid and why you can't be more like him. If you're a player and you are reading this, you are saying, Amen, Mr. Austin is right about now.

Once the family is secured in the vehicle and the engine is turned on, the fun starts. The ride home can go in several different directions. The first and most common direction is the one-way monologue. That is when the parent does all of the talking. The parent lectures the kid from the beginning of the ride all the way up to when the car is pulling into the driveway at home. Only one voice is heard the entire time and that is the parent's voice. Some speak in a civil tone while others may raise their voices a little more as they get more emotional and frustrated about what just happened in the game. Sometimes, the parent will stop lecturing the kid and just start ranting and raving to nobody in particular.

The next scenario is the dialogue in which the kid has

something to say in defense of himself. This can get interesting at times. It could lead to a good discussion between the two parties as they break down the game in a civil manner. But usually, the parent does not want to have his monologue interrupted and he might take the kid's protestations as a sign of disrespect. That's when the bickering begins between parent and child.

The third and most intriguing scenario of the dreaded ride home is when the second parent decides to get involved in the conversation. This opens up the ride home to several new possibilities, which could lead to some very entertaining banter. It all depends on what direction the second parent wants to take it. There are three popular themes to this scenario.

The first is the defense of the child which can be music to the kid's ears. The second parent decides that the first parent has said enough and now it's time to back off. Leave the kid alone. He feels bad enough already. Or the second parent can go right into attack mode and start to argue with the first parent about the treatment of the child. That's when things can get really heated as a big argument ensues between the two parents with the kid stuck in the middle.

The second parent can also step in and change the subject. It's a more diplomatic way of saying, "Enough already." The parent decides that enough time has been spent on this game and it's time to move on to something else. Let's turn the page. When the second parent turns on the radio, that's also a good sign that the subject is about to change.

The third and final theme is the worse possible scenario for the child. It's the infamous double-team. That's when the second parent starts to co-sign everything that the first parent is saying about you. Now, instead of one parent giving you the business, you now have both parents barking at you from all directions. As Michael Jackson used to sing as the scarecrow in the movie, The Wiz, "You Can't Win," you really can't say anything because you are really outnumbered when both Mom and Dad are unloading on you. All you can do is sit there and take it with the look on your face that says, "If looks could kill, I would be an orphan right about now."

The final scene to the dreaded ride home is complete silence. Nobody says anything. The car is completely quiet, but it will take a chainsaw to cut through all the tension in the air. Sometimes, that can be worse than the all-out bickering because Lord only knows what everyone is thinking at that particular moment.

What can be very helpful during these times of distress for the kid is the presence of a younger sibling in the car. The younger the sibling the better it is for you. You can always count on the baby brother or sister to say or do something that will divert all of the attention away from the drama of the dreaded ride home. Little people have that gift of grabbing the attention and boy do they come in handy at this time. When I was in high school, my younger brother Richard was still a toddler and he was also a ham. Perfect. When things would take a turn for the worse in the car, my baby brother would always provide some kind of levity to lighten up the situation.

My own "Dreaded Ride Home" moment occurred in 1981 at the beginning of my senior year as a basketball player at McCluer North High. We had just lost to our rival, McCluer High, in the championship game of their pre-season tournament and I did not play well. On the drive home, my father started to lecture me on my sub-par performance that night. He was dutifully pointing out my mistakes as well as my lack of effort and intensity. To be honest, I was cool with it because I deserved it. We had just lost to our rival school and I was not happy about how I played.

Unfortunately, my mother was not cool with what she was hearing. She was fiercely loyal to her kids and did not like anyone talking bad about them, including her husband; the father of her kids. Remember Scenario #3 in the dreaded ride home; the intervention of the second parent. My mother invoked the defense card on this night and she did it with great gusto and intensity. After about ten minutes of my father's lecture, my mother decided that she had heard enough. She interrupted my father and began to read him the riot act about how he was talking to her child; it did not matter that I was also his child. She must have hit my father with about fifty curse words during her tirade. She called my father just about every name in the book.

My father tried to calm her down, but she was having none of it. It only intensified her anger at my father. In her mind, somebody was trying to attack her baby boy, so it was on and poppin'. It was quite a show. It took all of the strength that my sister and I could muster not to bust out laughing. It was quite funny, but we just could not disrespect out father like that by laughing in his face. Not even my brother Richard could help the situation. Even at three years old, he was smart enough to know that when Mama got on a roll it was best for him to keep quiet and stay the hell out of her way. Sorry Dad, you're on your own.

Anyway, that is my "Dreaded Ride Home" testimonial. I know each of you have one as well and I would love to hear yours. These rides are still commonplace today, but I have to admit that today's kids are more prepared for the ride home than people of my generation were. They are smarter and more sophisticated than we were.

Thank God for iPods. They have become kids one great salvation and an escape on the ride home from the game.

We did not have that when I was playing. We just had to sit there and take the verbal beat down, or jump out of a moving car, risking life and limb.

Today, it is different for kids and I see it all the time. As soon as they get in the car, those headphones are immediately put on and their heads are bobbing up and down to the music which I'm sure is turned up very loudly. That's called beating Mom and Dad to the punch.

Other kids simply just jump in the car with their teammate and their parents. "Mom, I'm going to ride home with Johnny and his parents. I'll see you later tonight." That kills two birds with one stone. First, you avoid the dreaded ride home with your own parents. Secondly, you save your friend from his own dreaded ride home because both of you will spend the ride home talking to each other. As they say in the beverage commercial, "BRILLIANT!" That is unless the parent is bound and determined to have their post-game comments heard and they respond with an "OH, NO YOU'RE NOT! YOU BETTER BRING YOUR BUTT OVER HERE AND GET IN THIS CAR!!"

One former girls' basketball standout I knew, took the direct approach to avoid any drama on the drive home. This young lady played on a team in the Parkway School District and her team had just lost a tough game to a district rival. As the parents waited outside the locker room for their daughters to come out, this young lady came out and made a bee-line straight for her father. Before he could get a word out, she pointed at him and said, "I don't want to hear one word from you on the way home tonight. You understand me?!" This girl knew her father was a veteran of the dreaded ride home wars and she laid the law down to her father before they even left the gymnasium. The father was completely unarmed. The father just nodded his head. Drama averted.

Kids, be aware of the "dreaded ride home." In addition, it might be a good idea to be prepared for the "dreaded ride to the game." Sometimes, that can be worse than the ride home from the game. This is when the parents try to overload their poor young child with a multitude of instructions on what to do during the game. "Now, remember to do this, do that and the other thing. And don't forget to cover your man, hit your free throws, box out and rebound, blah, blah, blah." They overwhelm their children with needless information when all the kid wants to do is get ready for the game. If it is a short ride to the game, it is probably worse because the parent is talking at a mile-a-minute because he wants to make sure he gets all of his instructions in before your arrival at the game. When you arrive at the game and you see a young child getting out of the vehicle looking pretty punch-drunk, you know they have been the subject of an intense pre-game lecture from an over-zealous parent.

My thirteen-year-old nephew, Robin Charles Thompson, is an unwilling participant of the dreaded ride to the game. On the way to his youth basketball games, he hears it from both of his parents, my sister Courtney, and her husband Robin. First, Courtney will take her turn giving Robin all of the technical instructions he needs, since she played basketball herself. Then my brother-in-law will take over. He's a football guy, so he's hitting little Robin with, "You have to be tough out there, son. Don't let nobody take your rebound from you, you hear me." They can be relentless.

And if that wasn't enough, my sister would insist on calling Uncle Earl on his cell phone on their way to the game. She would put me on speaker and ask for me to talk to Robin and give him even more pre-game instructions. Young Robin is polite as he says, "Yes, Uncle Earl." But I know that sometimes in his mind, he has to be saying, "Will these crazy people just leave me alone?"

Sometimes, carpooling may be your best option.

*If you have a dreaded ride home story of your own from an activity, send it to Earl Austin Jr. at eaustin@stlamerican.com.

STRAITJACKET PARENT STORIES

You might need a jacket—

When you spend a lot of money to have bobblehead dolls made in the likeness of your child while she is still in high school, you might need a jacket.

One of my favorite high school girls' basketball players was a young lady who played for a school in South County during the early part of this decade. She was a tremendous shooter from the three-point line as well as from the free-throw line. She was automatic. This young lady was one of the most tenacious competitors in St. Louis. The girl was little, but she never backed down from a challenge. As a senior, she led her team on an improbable run to the district championship.

When the young lady was a senior in high school, her mother came up with a unique idea to celebrate her daughter's success. She wanted to have bobblehead dolls made in the girl's likeness, to give as a present to friends and family members. When the mother brought up the idea to her husband, he balked at the notion because it was pretty expensive. It would cost more than $2,000 to have the bobblehead dolls made and shipped. The husband put his foot down and said no. End of story—or so he thought.

As I said, the young lady was as tough as they come on the basketball court. It was a trait that she got from her mother, who is known to be feisty, strong-willed and independent. She is one who does not take no for an answer, especially when it comes to her youngest child.

Anyway, about a month later, a UPS truck showed up at the family home with a special delivery. Inside the box was a shipment of bobblehead dolls.

By the way, I received one of those dolls. Here it is.

****

You might need a jacket—

When you repeatedly bang your head against a door in an effort to get into the referee's room at your child's hockey game, and you end up knocking yourself unconscious, you are in need of a jacket.

Youth hockey games seem to be a good source for straitjacket parent stories. At one youth hockey tournament in St. Peters, Missouri, two of the players got into a fight and were kicked out of the game by the referee. The father of one of the ejected players was furious at the referee. After the game, the father headed to the room where the referees were for a post-game confrontation. However, the door to the room was closed and locked. Undaunted, the father rammed himself against the door headfirst in an effort to get it open. On the fourth try, the father managed to knock the door open, but in the process he also knocked himself out. By the time the other parents got to him, he was laid out on the floor, unconscious.

****

You might need a jacket—

When you make your own school flags to wave at your child's high school games, you might need a jacket.

One particular woman had three sons who were all high school basketball standouts at two of the top Catholic schools in the area. She cheered her boys' every move with great enthusiasm, but she took her support one step further. The mother had a friend who was a seamstress, and she had that woman sew school flags so she could wave them at her sons' games. When I first saw the woman with her flag, I told her I thought it was cool that the school would allow a parent to wave the school flag at a game. She corrected me and told me that it was her own flag which she had made herself. Oh, excuse me. When her youngest son transferred to a rival school in the area, she had another flag made in the new school colors which she proudly waved as her son led his team to the state championship.

****

You might need a jacket—

When you go into the huddle of your child's team during a time-out, you might need a jacket.

Keeping it in the same family, the father of the aforementioned trio of basketball standouts was known for his great intensity. It helped make him a high school basketball star on the South Side back in the late 1960's. He instilled that same intensity in his sons, who all went on to have successful high school and college careers in athletics. Well, the father's intensity, as well as his curiosity, got the best of him one night during one son's high school game. When the team coach called a time-out, the father wandered over and joined his son and his teammates in the huddle to find out what was going on. Really, he did! I don't think he was too welcomed in the huddle.

During another game, this father was so loud in his protest against the officiating referee that he got the attention of one referee, who turned toward the coach and gave him a technical foul. Since the dad was sitting close to the coach, the official had thought it was the coach who was yelling at him, so he whistled him for the technical. The stunned coach pointed out the father to the referee and let him know that he, the coach, was innocent, and that the overzealous father was the culprit doing all the yelling.

****

You might need a jacket—

When you are arrested and led away from your child's football game in handcuffs after being tasered by a police officer, you definitely need a jacket.

This incident took place at a football game for eight-year-olds in O'Fallon, Missouri. It made national headlines. One father was on the sidelines during the football game, and his brother joined him there. Both brothers became angry at a call made by the referee. They started cursing at the referee and shoving other parents, who were trying to calm them down. One of those parents happened to be an off-duty sheriff's deputy who also had a son on the team. This father responded to the ruckus by taking out his taser gun and dropping one of the brothers. While the man was one the ground, the other brother continued to bark at the deputy, as well as at another off-duty officer on the scene. Despite pleas from other parents to stop his tirade because of all the young children present, the man continued with his loud theatrics. Both brothers were eventually arrested and taken away in handcuffs. The whole scene was captured on video by the grandfather of another player, who had the camera rolling the entire time.

****

You might need a jacket—

When you create your own coaching box opposite your child's bench during his basketball games, you might need a jacket.

During the late 1990's, an uncle of a player from Webster Groves High would show up early at the gymnasium for each game, and he would always sit across from the Statesmen's bench and coach the team. I'm not sure if the kids were paying attention to him, since there already was a head coach in place who had actually been hired to do the job. But this didn't matter to the uncle. He was in his own little glory, living out his dream.

While we were watching this fan in action at the Meramec Tournament, Randy Carter, the Jennings coach, walked into the gym to scout the game, and we started talking about the Webster fan who was coaching his nephew's team from across the floor. Randy proceeded to tell us a story about the father of one of his former players, who used to come to the Warriors games early with a roll of duct tape. The father would use the tape to create his own coaching box across from the Jennings bench, and from there he'd yell instructions to the players for the entire game. By the way, nobody else was allowed in this coaching box during the game. That's quite bold, I must say.

****

You might need a jacket—

When you throw a milk shake at the referees at your son's hockey game, you just might need a jacket.

A woman was watching her son play in a local youth hockey tournament for eleven and twelve-year-olds. Her son was called for a penalty on a play and banished to the penalty box. The mother was not happy with the official who called the penalty, and she showed her displeasure by taking a strawberry milk shake and throwing it over the glass at the referee. The milk shake missed its intended target; it landed on the ice and exploded on impact, causing a big mess. The game was delayed for several minutes while the mess was cleaned up. Meanwhile, the mother was escorted out of the game by the local sheriff's department.

****

You might need a jacket—

When you call a radio talk show every day to criticize your child's coach, you might need a jacket.

During the early 1990's, a parent of a player from one of the area's top high school basketball programs used to call Richard "Onion" Horton's radio talk show on WGNU every morning. The parent would get on the air and rip his son's coach on everything from game strategy to substitution patterns, his son's playing time and anything else he could think of. The man's scathing criticisms knew no boundaries. He was relentless in his verbal assaults on his son's coach— on live radio.

****

You might need a jacket—

When you keep your own personal statistics on your child during a game, you might need a jacket.

I have found this to be a common theme among straitjacket parents. In fact, if I had a dollar for every parent I've seen keeping personal statistics on his or her son or daughter, I would have enough money to help solve some of this country's economic problems. These parents show up at the games with their little notebooks and keep track of only one player: their kid. Some of them have gone as far as going to the official scorer's table after the game to make sure that their numbers added up with the numbers in the official scorebook. If not, they would try to change the numbers in the official book. Such parents are convinced that their numbers are correct and the official scorebook is wrong. They'll do anything for that extra point or rebound that will enhance the stat sheet.

The most thorough personal stat-keeper for his child was a well-known former local high school and college coaching legend. He would sit up at the top of the bleachers and chart every one of his son's shots. It was pretty sophisticated stuff. The man would chart where his son's shots came from, at what point in the game he took them, and what kind of shots he took. Not only did he chart these shots during the game, he also kept track of every shot his son took during pre-game warm-ups. When he got home, he would leave the notebook on the kitchen table for his son to read over if he wanted to. This coach had always paid keen attention to detail; in this case, it might have been a little too much. Yes, local coaching legends can find their way into a jacket.

****

You might need a jacket—

When you get kicked out of your child's game on Senior Night, you might need a jacket.

At high school games, Senior Night is a special night not only for the senior athletes who receive special recognition, but for their parents. It is their one opportunity to come out on the basketball court or football field and receive their own recognition as they escort their kids onto the playing field.

This particular incident took place several years ago at the girls' basketball game at McCluer High School. One parent was so intense in his protest at the official that he wound up being ejected from the gym before the actual ceremony, which was to be held at halftime. When halftime rolled around, the school officials went outside, found the father and brought him back inside the gym so he could escort his daughter onto the court. After the ceremony, he was promptly escorted back out of the gym for the rest of the game. Poor guy!

****

You might need a jacket—

When a school's student cheering section has its own special cheer for you, you might need a jacket.

Student cheering sections are quite common at high school events. They love to razz the opposing team's players and coaches, and sometimes the opposing student sections. Rarely, however, do they turn their attention to the parent of a player from the opposing school.

I saw this happen for the first time several years ago, when I went to see a big game between two top high school teams. The father in question was a local sports celebrity, and his son was one of the area's top players. The dad was a most enthusiastic advocate for his son. During this game, which was for the conference championship, the son dribbled through the lane and attempted a layup. He was fouled on the play, but there was no whistle. As the action continued, the father immediately jumped up and started to protest that the foul wasn't called.

Seeing the father hollering at the officials from across the court, the student section from the rival school jumped up and broke out with the cheer, "Daddy's angry!" Clap-clap-clap-clap-clap, "Daddy's angry!"

Now, that's creative!

****

You might need a jacket—

When you yell at your kid to take all the shots and never pass the ball to his or her teammates, you might need a jacket.

This is another common theme among straitjacket parents. It gets even worse when the father happens to be the coach of the team. One father I knew who coached a youth basketball team ran virtually every play so that his son would shoot the ball. I wound up giving him the nickname "Press," after Press Maravich, who coached his son "Pistol" Pete Maravich during his college career at LSU, when Pete set all the NCAA scoring records during the late 1960's. Pistol Pete shot all the balls at LSU, as did this man's young son.

****

You might need a jacket—

When you try to coach your child's team from behind the team bench, drowning out the actual coach, who is trying to give his own instructions, you might need a jacket.

A local former professional athlete and his wife have raised four terrific student athletes, who have all gone on to participate in NCAA Division I Athletics. While his kids were in high school, the father was one of the most enthusiastic and intense parents that you will ever find—anywhere!

During one night, when his oldest son's team was playing its city rival in the first round of the regional playoffs, the father and the rest of the family took their seats near the top of the bleachers. The team was one of the top seeds in the tournament and an easy favorite to take care of their cross town rivals. Well, the underdog rivals scored the first ten points of the game which sparked early talk of a shocking upset in the making. This was more than the father could take. As Popeye would say, he could not stands no more!

Within seconds, the father made his way down from the top of the bleachers to directly behind his son's team bench, where he started yelling instructions and coaching the team himself. He was pacing up and down the sidelines while instructing his son's team. Meanwhile, the head coach calmly went about his business of coaching the team, seemingly oblivious of the commotion behind him. This went on for virtually the entire first half. Only when his son's team started to take control of the game did the father begin to calm down and take a seat. My mouth was wide open with amazement as I watched this scene play itself out. It was beautiful to watch. And I had a front-row seat to all of it!

****

You might need a jacket—

When you are escorted from your child's basketball game in handcuffs, you most certainly need a jacket.

This happened at a high school basketball game between Belleville Althoff and Quincy (Ill.) at the 2003 Collinsville Holiday Tournament. Now, there may not be a more hardcore group of basketball fans than the brood from Quincy. The program has great tradition, and the fans love their Blue Devils. Boy, do they ever love their Blue Devils! When the Quincy folks start to come after the referees, they come after them with feeling and passion.

In this hotly contested game, Althoff began to pull away in the fourth quarter. As each second counted down, you could see Blue Devil Nation becoming unhinged. The head coach of the team fanned the flames of discontent by getting whistled for two technical fouls and being ejected from the game. With the game out of reach, the fans turned their anger to the officials, unleashing a full-throated verbal assault on the men in stripes.

One referee had enough. He turned to an older gentleman who was really going strong and kicked him out of the game. As the old man began to leave, he was followed out of the building by a legion of Quincy fans. All of them had something to say to the official as they filed out of Virgil Fletcher Gymnasium in disgust. However, one particular parent was not in a hurry to leave, and he continued to bark at anyone who cared to listen. For his over-the-top efforts, he received a pair of handcuffs and a personal escort out of the building, courtesy of the Collinsville Police Department. They really, really take their high school basketball seriously in Quincy, Ill!

****

You might need a jacket—

When you show up drunk at your child's games, you will need not only a jacket but also a cab ride home. This is not a pretty sight.

I've seen this happen a few times over the years, and you really feel for the kid in such a situation, especially when the parent gets really, really loud and obnoxious Just picture the scene from the movie Hoosiers, in which the character Shooter, played by Dennis Hopper, shows up drunk at a game and totally embarrasses himself and his son.

****

You might need a jacket—

When you take your eight-year-old son to seventeen different basketball camps during one summer, you might need a jacket.

Several years ago, a father took his second-grade son to seventeen different basketball camps during one summer. That's right, seventeen. I know this for a fact because I saw the actual list. The father showed it to me. We were at a basketball camp at McCluer North, and I saw his son playing. He was very good for his age, dominating the competition, and everyone at the camp took notice. The boy became quite the little celebrity that week, as he continued to put on a show.

At the end of the week, the kid's father came up to me and asked, "How do you like my son, Mr. Austin?" I told him he was a very good player with a bright future. The father proceeded to whip out a sheet of paper with a list of all the camps he'd taken his son to that summer and those he would still participate in. The list looked rather extensive, so out of curiosity I counted the camps. There turned out to be seventeen.

"Seventeen camps?" I asked. "Why so many?"

The man had a simple explanation for his son's city-wide tour: "My wife wanted me to put him in daycare for the summer, but it was too expensive. I went to several different places, but I could not afford it, so I thought I would just take him to basketball camps. He would have fun, he would be taken care of, and it does not cost a lot of money. So we just went from basketball camp to basketball camp."

Today the young man is one of the area's top point guards. And the father continues to be one of the most enthusiastic parents going.

****

You might need a jacket—

When you send threatening e-mails to your child's coach, you might need a jacket. This is another common theme. Sometimes advanced technology is not a good thing.

****

You might need a jacket—

When you transfer your child to four different high schools in four years, you might need a jacket—and a small amount of patience. Some people are hard to please, I guess.

Let's see. If my math is correct, that's one school per year. That's what this father did to his daughter. She was a pretty good high school basketball player. The problem was, she never got a chance to stay in one place long enough to display her talent. For one reason or another, her father was never happy with her school situation, so off he went to a new school, along with his daughter. The sad part about the whole deal was that the state association declared the young lady ineligible to play for her senior year. One of the schools she attended had reported her to the state, costing the girl her senior year of competition on the basketball court.

Another father went one step further with his son. He got so transfer-happy that his son attended five different high schools in three cities and two states. He spent his freshman year at two different schools on the West Coast. He then moved to the Midwest, where he attended one school and then transferred to another school in another part of the state. When that didn't work out, the father moved across the state again, to put his son in his fifth school in four years.

****

You might need a jacket—

If you are a school administrator and you berate a teacher who has reprimanded your child for a transgression, you might need a jacket.

Yes, a school administrator can get caught up as well. This particular woman had a child who was a star athlete at the same school where she was vice-principal. When the athlete got involved in a little horseplay in class, he was reprimanded by the teacher and he wound up being suspended for a game. When the vice-principal found out about what had happened to her son, she did not want to talk to the kid to discuss his wrongdoing. Instead, she called the teacher into her office and read him the riot act. She verbally thrashed him up one side and down the other. How dare this man discipline her son and cause him to miss a game? She even threatened to have the poor teacher fired. Wow!

****

You might need a jacket—

When you get on an Internet message board to publicly criticize your child's coach, you might need a jacket.

The father of a local college basketball star went onto the school's unofficial message board and started criticizing his son's coach. The poor dad's action made local and national headlines.

****

You might need a jacket—

When you get on an Internet message board to argue with other chat-room posters who are criticizing your child's performance, you might need a jacket.

This father became addicted to the college basketball chat rooms. His son was one of the area's top players, and he signed early with one of the local schools. The father became a regular poster on that school's basketball chat room. Things were all lovey-dovey between the father and the other posters, as he kept them up to date on how things were going during his son's senior year.

However, when the young man experienced some tough times on the court in college, the chat-room posters turned on him and began to ridicule him. That's the bad thing about chat rooms: the posters are protected by their anonymity, so they feel like they can say whatever they want. They said some rough stuff about his young man, much to his father's chagrin. His natural instinct was to protect his son, so he fired back at the posters which caused a lot of friction at times. Some heated exchanges took place in the chat room. In the meantime, the father became obsessed with the chat room. He spent much of his life in front of the computer, and the constant criticism of his son took its toll on him.

Said his daughter, "He needed to take blood pressure medicine because of all the stress from that computer."

****

You might need a jacket—

When it becomes your hobby to blast people on chat boards about your kids' sports, you may need a jacket. Memo to parents: Stay away from those chat rooms! You might not always like what is written about your children. There are people who post on chat rooms who are not very nice.

Another Internet message-board scene took place several years ago, when the father of a young man became unhinged after his son was cut from a summer basketball team. The father went on a message board and started blasting one of the coaches of the team, calling him names and abusing him with numerous personal attacks. When the coach finally went on the message board to defend himself, the father called him out in an all-out Internet confrontation. Reportedly, school administrators had to get involved on the coach's behalf.

****

You might need a jacket—

When you and your spouse cannot sit together at your kid's games, one of you might need a jacket.

I see this all the time. My parents never sat together at my games. Their personalities were too different. My mother was the loud one and my father was the quiet one. It worked out quite well.

I saw another great example of this while watching the championship game of a Women's Conference basketball tournament in Charlotte, back in March. A young lady was helping her team win the tournament title, and her parents were getting a lot of face time on television. It was the best. Her mother was in the school's cheering section, having a great time, waving her pom-poms and taking pictures of her daughter. Meanwhile, the player's father was sitting in his seat near the top of the arena all by himself. Nobody was around him. It was a great study in contrast, seeing how different parents approach their kids' games.

****

You might need a jacket—

When you move your star athlete child from town A to town B to play high school sports at the beginning of his career, and then you move your family back to town A after he graduates from the school in town B, you might need a jacket. This scenario happened in Illinois several years ago. Now, that is a parent with some real guts.

****

You might need a jacket—

If you are the wife of a basketball coach and you constantly get into heated arguments with parents and fans at basketball games, you might need a jacket.

Coaches' wives know how to mix it up, as well. The wife of a former high school coach in South County did not take kindly to parents or any other fans who criticized her husband during the game. If she heard anyone sitting in her vicinity criticize her husband, she would not hesitate to get in that person's face and confront him or her. Now, that's called loyalty. Stand by your man! Tammy Wynette would be proud. Yes, the wives of coaches are eligible for jackets.

****

You might need a jacket—

If you are coaching a high school basketball team that is scheduled to play in a summer tournament, and you cancel the tournament for the entire team because your kid does not want to play that weekend, you might need a jacket.

A few years back, a local coach had scheduled his team to play in a summer tournament in the Chicago area. The team was all set to go, but then the coach's son decided that he did not feel like going on the trip. Instead of leaving his son behind and taking the rest of the team to Chicago to play, the coach decided to cancel the entire trip to Chi-Town. Now, who is running that family?

****

You might need a jacket—

When you and your family members start a post-game brawl with your child's coach, all of you need jackets.

This wild scene took place several years ago. After a game, the mother of one of the players confronted the coach in an angry manner. Pretty soon a full-scale brawl broke out, complete with aunts, uncles, siblings, parents and assistant coaches. It was a scene straight out of "The Jerry Springer Show." Straitjackets all around on this one.

****

You might need a jacket—

If you shop your junior high school child around to different high schools as if he or she were a commodity, you might need a jacket.

It can get pretty unseemly when parents start shopping their twelve and thirteen-year-old children around to different high schools, acting like they are sports agents and their kids are their special commodities.

****

You might need a jacket—

When you try to attack a professional boxer in the middle of a fight in which he is whipping the daylights out of your son, you might need a jacket.

East St. Louis native Arthur "Flash" Johnson enjoyed an excellent amateur and professional boxing career. He even fought for a world title. Near the end of his career, Johnson started promoting his own shows and putting them on in his hometown. During one fight I attended, Johnson was pummeling his opponent from pillar to post during the first round of this main-event bout. As Johnson sat on his stool between rounds, I noticed two women advance angrily toward his corner. Both were yelling and cursing at Johnson. It turned out to be the mother and sister of Johnson's opponent. They wanted a piece of Arthur for what he was doing to their poor son and brother.

This incident was reminiscent of that famous scene that took place during a professional bout in England, when in the middle of a fight the mother of one of the fighters actually got into the ring and started attacking her son's opponent with her shoe. That has to be one of the best straitjacket parent moments of all time.

****

You might need a jacket—

If you are a Little League Baseball coach and you have a baseball uniform of your own, you definitely need a jacket.

I could be wrong here, but I think it's pretty silly for a Little League coach to have his own uniform. There should be league rules against this sort of insanity. Who do you think you are, Whitey Herzog? The first time I saw this was at a Little League game several years ago, while I was helping out my father's team. We saw this coach with his team of eight-year-olds, and he was decked out in his own uniform, head to toe. My father and I both fell over laughing.

****

You might need a jacket—

If you try to shoot a teenage umpire at a Little League Baseball game, you most certainly need a jacket—and a little jail time, to boot.

Sadly, this incident took place at a ballpark in the Metro East area. A man became so unbalanced at his kid's Little League game that he got out his gun and started shooting at a sixteen-year-old umpire because the umpire had called the man's nine-year-old son out at the plate. The team was trailing by one run, and the umpire's call nullified the game-tying run. This sent the gun-toting straitjacket coach into a tizzy. Luckily, the coach was not a good shot and he missed the kid. He was also arrested. Anyway, why on earth would somebody bring a gun to a Little League Baseball game?

****

You might need a jacket—

When your child can hear your voice over thousands of others at a crowded sporting event, you might need a jacket—and a muzzle.

****

You might need a jacket—

When you criticize your own sibling throughout an entire game, you might need a jacket.

This jacket belongs to me, Earl Austin Jr. Yes, the easygoing, laid-back person you all know and love has experienced a few moments of straitjacket behavior in his past. During my sister Courtney's college basketball career at Lindenwood University, I used to ride her mercilessly from the stands at all her games.

When Courtney was a freshman, I was the assistant coach of the women's team. During one game in which she wasn't playing too well, I took her aside during a time-out and told her to get her head out of her (expletive) and start playing to her potential. Courtney reminds me of this incident all the time and she would not rest until I put it in this book.

For her next two years, I became the men's assistant coach, so I could watch her games as a fan instead of a coach. I admit to being a little crazy at times. Every mistake she made, I would stand up and start yelling at her,

"Courtney, stop fouling!" "Courtney, get your hands up!" "Courtney, use the backboard!" I didn't realize how much of a fool I was making of myself.

Finally, I got the message late in her junior year, when I read an article about Courtney in the St. Charles Post newspaper that talked about her following in my footsteps as a basketball standout at Lindenwood. In the articles, Courtney mentioned how seriously I took basketball. She said something like, "Basketball is life or death with my brother, but it isn't with me. I like to shop." That's when I realized that we were different people, and there was nothing wrong with that. We both had great careers at Lindenwood, even though our approaches to the game were not the same. I loved the game and was consumed by it twenty-four hours a day. While Courtney also loved to play, she had other interests off the court. Once I came to grips with that, I toned down my act during her senior year, and she had the best year of her career. She is now in Lindenwood's Hall of Fame.

****

You might need a jacket—

When your child volunteers to write a big essay that chronicles your crazy behavior during his games, you might need a jacket.

At a summer basketball tournament last summer in North County, I was talking to some of the players, who were telling me little stories about their own parents' brushes with straitjacket greatness. That was when one player came up to me and said, "Mr. Austin, I can write a ten-page essay on how my father behaves at the games." As I said in the introduction, even the kids are quick to drop a dime on their parents.

****

You might need a jacket—

If you almost injure one of your children while cheering for your other child, you might need a jacket.

My sister, Courtney, has three sons, who all participate in youth sports, so she is a straitjacket parent-in-training. While she was cheering for her older son, Robin, at one of his basketball games, her younger son, Austin, was resting on her lap. In the game's closing seconds, Robin got an offensive rebound and put in the game-winning basket. Courtney started jumping up and down, yelling for Robin. In the process of celebrating, she forgot that Austin was hanging onto her. As she jumped, Austin went flying. He landed on the floor and rolled a couple of feet onto the court. Although a bit stunned, the little guy was fine.

****

You might need a jacket—

When you follow your child down the sidelines while he is running for a touchdown during a football game, you might need a jacket.

Once again, my sister is front and center. This scene happened during one of Austin's football games. Austin, who is nine years old, is a pretty good little quarterback. During his last game of the season, Austin broke loose for an eighty-yard touchdown run. Running along beside Austin every step of the way on the sidelines was Courtney, screaming at the top of her lungs.

"You're darn right I was excited," Courtney explained. "I couldn't believe it was Austin. He looked like a baby Gale Sayers."

My brother-in-law, Robin, who coaches the team, found the scene quite amusing. "It was hilarious," he said. "I'm trying to watch my son run for this touchdown, but I'm also looking at my wife running with him."

****

You might need a jacket—

When you start an Internet Web site for your child before his or her high school career even begins, you might need a jacket.

One of our area's top basketball players was well-known before he entered high school. One reason for this was that he was a talented young player. Another reason was that his father, who is in the computer field, started a Web site dedicated to his son.

****

You might need a jacket—

When you are banned from attending your child's home games, you need a jacket. That's pretty strong stuff, right there.

****

37

You might need a jacket—

When you get into a fight with your ex-wife's new boyfriend at your child's athletic event, you might need a jacket.

This man got into a heated altercation with his ex-wife's new boyfriend in the parking lot of his kid's game several years ago. Let it go, man! Let it go.

****

You might need a jacket—

When you and your team members attack a referee at a basketball game, all of you need jackets.

This sad event happened at a youth basketball tournament in North County several years ago. The young official was knocked unconscious by the coach and then summarily hit with a chair as he lay motionless on the court. Terrible!

****

You might need a jacket—

If you have never missed one of your kid's practices during his or her high school career, you might need a jacket—and a life!

It's one thing never to miss a game, but never to miss a practice! In the words of Allen Iverson, "We're not talking about games, we're talking about practice." This was a parent who truly had a lot of time on his hands.

YOU MIGHT NEED A JACKET

****

You might need a jacket—

If you are a small-town police sergeant, and you send two of your officers to the home of a junior college basketball player to intimidate and harass her in order to settle a beef the girl had with your daughter, who plays on the same team, you might need a jacket.

Not even the law is immune to straitjacket-parenthood. I read about this scenario in the St. Louis Post-Dispatch newspaper last year, in a column by Sylvester Brown. When a master sergeant from the Illinois State Police Department learned of a pre-game shoving match his daughter had had with her teammate at a local junior college, he responded to the incident by getting the address of his daughter's rival and sending a couple of his officers over to her house for a little ol' fashioned intimidation. The two officers reportedly threatened the girl with jail time for her role in the incident and warned her to stay away from Sarge's daughter. One can only imagine what had to be going through the mind of the nineteen-year-old girl, who had had a season-long beef with the sergeant's daughter, culminating in this pre-game shoving match. The young lady's mother reported the incident to the Illinois state authorities. The young lady, who played high school basketball in St. Louis, has since transferred to another school.

That's quite disturbing.

****

You might need a jacket—

If you are the wife of a basketball official who is running

a referees' camp at a basketball tournament, your child is playing in the tournament, and you constantly berate the officials your husband is trying to evaluate, you might need a jacket.

Each year, a summer basketball tournament is held in St. Louis in conjunction with a referees' organization. The games are officiated by referees who are being evaluated for future assignments. One of the chief evaluators at the camp had a son playing in the tournament. Whenever this man's son's team was playing, his wife was on the referee's case all throughout the game. Imagine being one of the young referees, and you're being evaluated by a head official, while at the same time his wife is giving you an earful every time you come down the court. What an interesting dynamic that was—and I was there to see it!

****

You might need a jacket—

When you tell a reporter that his newspaper sucks because he will not write a feature article on your child, you might need a jacket.

That's all part of the job, my good people. All parents want a little recognition for their children, and that's a good thing. One mother sat down next to me at a basketball tournament and asked me why I hadn't done an article on her son's high school. I told her the team wasn't doing so well that year. She then went on about how her son was doing well even though the team was terrible. I quickly figured out that she really did not care that I had not written an article on the school; she only wanted something written about her son. After about five minutes, she'd had enough. She just said, "Mr. Austin, your newspaper sucks. It just sucks. It really sucks!" I could only laugh.

I've also had a mother of a child who attended school in St. Louis County tell me that the only reason I did not write an article on her son was because there was a conspiracy in the St. Louis City Government not to feature kids from St. Louis County in our newspaper, because the city wanted to put an end to the voluntary desegregation program, and I was part of that conspiracy against the county athletes. She was dead serious.

One grandmother threatened to hit me with her cane because I momentarily forgot to mention her grandson at an athletic awards banquet that I was hosting.

I've also had a parent blame me for his child not getting a Division I Basketball scholarship because I didn't publicize the kid enough—despite the fact that the young man had averaged barely five points a game.

In twenty-two years, you hear just about everything. Those are only a few of the highlights.

****

You might need a jacket—

If you are not satisfied with your child's playing time on his football team, and you decide to get in your car and follow the coach home for a confrontation, you deserve to have a jacket—custom-made.

My brother-in-law coaches a youth football team in North County. A few years back, he had one straitjacket parent who was never satisfied with his son's role on the team. He wanted his son to have more carries, despite the fact that the boy carried the ball more than any other player on the team. During one game, the father left the field in a huff and wound up missing his son scoring the game-winning touchdown. Near the end of the season, this father decided to get in his car and follow my brother-in-law out of the park after a game. This could have been dangerous. My brother-in-law really did not figure it out until he noticed a car following him from turn to turn. He decided to pull into the parking lot of a nearby restaurant. Then he got out of the car and went to the driver of the car that was following him, to find out what his problem was. After my brother-in-law gave the father a few choice words about his actions, the father backed down and left the parking lot. By the way, the kid was no longer on the team.

****

You might need a jacket—

When you throw a football helmet at your son's team coach, you might need a jacket

****

You might need a jacket—

When you go out on the basketball court in the middle of a high school game and punch the referee, you are a prime candidate for a jacket.

Yes, this happened at a New Haven-Pacific High School basketball game during the 2008 season. Right in front of everybody.

****

You might need a jacket—

When you threaten to kill your grandson's coach after he kicks the young lad off the team, you deserve a jacket.

A local basketball coach had more problems than he could stand with one of his players, so he wound up removing him from the team. The young man had a pair of straitjacket parents, who were a constant thorn in his side. However, the coup-de-grace came when the child's grandfather paid the coach a visit. After a few minutes of heated discussion, dear old Granddad burst out, "If you mess with my grandson again, I'm going to kill you!"

Welcome to the club, Grandpa.

****

You might need a jacket—

When you are kicked out of your child's game, and as you are leaving the gymnasium, you throw food and soda at the school's trophy case, you might need a jacket.

This scene took place at the Visitation Girls' Basketball Tournament a few years back. Mom was not happy about getting the heave-ho from the officials. For good measure, she was also banned from her daughter's home games at her school later that season.

****

You might need a jacket—

When you call the coach at home late at night in an

43

attempt to have your child's statistics changed from that night's game, you might need a jacket.

****

You might need a jacket—

When you attempt to embellish the truth about the colleges that are recruiting your child in order to make yourself look good, you may need a jacket.

It seems like every parent longs for the day when his son or daughter receives that college scholarship offer from one of the big-time universities around the country. It's a big boost to the ego when you can tell your friends that your child has received an offer to play football at Ohio State or basketball at North Carolina. This gets really murky when the parents start making up stories about who is actually recruiting their children.

One incident that comes to mind is when I was eating at a local restaurant, and the woman who managed the place came over to me to tell me about her son, whom I had watched play basketball several times. She came to me, very excited, and said, "Mr. Austin, my son just received a scholarship offer from Georgia Tech! I'm so excited."

I just smiled and said, "Congratulations." All the while, I was saying to myself, "There's no way her son is being recruited by an Atlantic Coast Conference school." He was only about five-foot-eight, and not very fast. He was a solid little high school player, but mom so wanted to believe that her son was headed to the Atlantic Coast Conference that she did not mind stretching the truth a little bit. This happens all the time.

Parents, just because you get a questionnaire from a school, it does not mean that your kid is being recruited by that school. There is nothing wrong with your child being recruited by smaller colleges or schools that are not on television every week.

The straitjacket parent behavior that goes on during the collegiate recruiting process can provide enough material for its own book. Parents can really go off the deep end during the recruiting process, especially if they have a child who is a special player and in great demand by the top programs.

****

You might need a jacket—

When you go into the huddle of the opposing team during a time-out and start yelling at the coach and players, you might need a jacket.

****

You might need a jacket—

When you join the coaching staff of your child's team as soon as he enters high school and you leave the staff when he graduates, you might need a jacket.

It has become quite common to see parents join the school's coaching staff when their standout children enter high school. One story in particular comes to mind. In 1992, a future McDonald's All-American guard made his high school debut at a local school. The young man's father decided to join the coaching staff as an assistant. At the

45

school's first home game, many of the family's friends were in attendance, as was I.

The one vivid memory I have from this evening was of the father coming out with a rolled-up program in his hands, wearing an old, stylish suit that had probably been sitting in his closet for twenty years. The father's friends started calling him Shooter, after Dennis Hopper's character in the movie Hoosiers. Shooter was the father of a player who joined the coaching staff in the middle of the season. When his son graduated, in 1995, Dad moved on. Many of his friends still call him Shooter.

****

You might need a jacket—

When your child is not voted captain of his team, and your response is to go up to the school, gather all the players together and demand another vote, you might need a jacket.

This scene was better than the 2000 presidential-election recount in Florida. Mom was really looking forward to seeing her son become the captain of his basketball team for his senior year. When the team voted for another player instead of her son, she went into action. She was at the school the following day, gathering the team together and demanding another vote.

****

You might need a jacket—

When you organize a group of parents in an effort to get your child's coach fired, you might need a jacket.

This is another common theme for straitjacket parents. There's strength in numbers. It gets real juicy in the smaller communities, when you have those town-hall meetings and barbershop gatherings. We had something similar happen in St. Louis a few years back. A group of parents got together and succeeded in getting their kids' high school basketball coach relieved of his duties. However, the coach fought back and ended up having the last laugh. He got a lawyer, fought the ruling and wound up getting his job back. The following year, at the school's basketball tryouts, the coach cut every player whose parent had had a hand in getting him fired.

****

You might need a jacket—

When you have your child repeat the eighth grade which in essence is a redshirt year, to enhance his or her chances of getting an athletic scholarship, you might need a jacket.

This has become a common practice, not only in St. Louis, but around the country. Parents are having their children repeat a grade, usually the eighth, at a different junior high school before starting their high school careers. It's similar to what colleges do when they "redshirt" athletes. The athletes are still on scholarship, but they don't play with the team; they spend the year getting bigger, stronger, and of course a little older. This is what usually happens during that second year of eighth-grade education.

Boy, times have changed! Back when I was in school, if a child had to repeat a grade, the kid usually wore the invisible scarlet D on his chest for being dumb.

Student cheering sections have started to get wise to

this process. Whenever they come across a player from the other team who has repeated the eighth grade, they hit him with the cheer of "Fifth-year senior!"-clap-clap-clap-clap-clap," or "Fourth-year junior!"

I have to say that this year-repeating maneuver has turned out to be smart on the parents' part. The kids who have done this have gone on to great high school careers and a very high level of college basketball.

****

You might need a jacket—

When you slap your child's coach in the face at a Summer League game, and the coach winds up calling the police and 911 on you after the incident, you might need a jacket.

During a Summer League girls' basketball game in West County a few years back, one father heard a coach saying some negative things about his daughter. He came down the bleachers, confronted the coach about the comments and ended up slapping the coach across the face. In sheer panic, the coach called the police and 911 on the angry dad.

****

You might need a jacket—

When you threaten your child's high school coach with a transfer to another school every week because things don't seem to go your way, you might need a jacket.

This particular father had a son who was the best player on his high school team as a freshman. Knowing that his son was the best player, the father felt he could bust the coach's chops any time he felt like it. He used the weapon of threatening to transfer the boy to another school whenever he didn't get his way. The man was relentless. "The coach won't let my son play his game...my son should be the point guard...my son should be getting more shots—we're going to transfer!" This went on for three years before the dad finally made good on his threat and transferred the kid to another school in the area. I could only imagine the coach's relief when this father finally took his son out of the school.

****

You might need a jacket—

When you are the father of a high school basketball coach and you get yourself kicked out of your son's game, you might need a jacket.

Yes, Lou Potsou, the man who coined the phrase "straitjacket parent" has been kicked out of two basketball games at Whitfield High, where his son Michael is the head coach. It takes one to know one!

****

You might need a jacket—

When you put your son through a two-hour workout after he has already played in a game, you might need a jacket.

Ronnie Dean, a long-time college and junior-college coach, was in Indianapolis watching his son Lezcano play in the Amateur Athletic Union National Tournament. On this particular evening, Ronnie was not pleased with how his son played. So, as everyone was clearing out of the gym, Ronnie kept Lezcano behind to conduct a personal post-game workout. The custodian at the local gym was sweeping the floor, trying to close things up and go home. He told Ronnie that it was late and he should go home. Ronnie responded by taking a hundred-dollar bill out of his wallet and throwing it on the floor in front of the custodian's broom. Ronnie told the custodian to take the money and get the hell out of the gym until he and his son had finished. Then he proceeded to put his tired son through a grueling two-hour workout. It was past midnight when the two of them finally left the gym.

****

You might need a jacket—

When you swing your purse and hit another woman in the face during an altercation in the parking lot after your children's rival teams play a game, you might need a jacket. Ladies, please! Calm down.

****

You might need a jacket—

When you are the coach of a youth basketball team, and you are wheelchair-bound, and to protest an official's call you wheel your chair onto the middle of the floor and try to run the official over, you might need a jacket.

This scene was part of one of the wildest youth basketball games I have ever witnessed. It took place at a tournament at Hazelwood East High, and it featured basketball players from the third grade. They were little guys out there, but the emotions were running so high that you would have thought Duke and North Carolina were playing for the national title. The parents on both sides were completely out of control. When they weren't yelling at the referees and their kids, they were screaming at each other.

Two parents from one of the teams were kicked out for yelling at the officials too much. One of these parents was a former local basketball standout, a rather low-key individual—but not on this day. This was only the beginning. Two more parents, one from each team, were at the scorer's table. One of them was keeping the scorebook, while the other was keeping the clock. He thought the first parent was trying to cheat on the score. They got into a shouting match and had to be separated before fisticuffs started. "I'm usually a low-key person, but not when it comes to my kids," the clock-watching parent explained. "They were trying to cheat my kids. And you don't cheat my kids!"

The capper was when the coach of one of the teams, who was in a wheelchair, got so upset with the officials that he motored his chair onto the court and tried to run the referee down. It was priceless.

****

You might need a jacket—

When you illegally play your child on a team for a younger age bracket in order to make him look good, you might need a jacket.

We saw this unscrupulous behavior on the national scene in 2001, when fourteen-year-old Danny Almonte became the star of the Little League World Series. The problem was, he was playing against eleven and twelve-year-olds. Totally bogus! This scenario has taken place in St. Louis, as well. One father was notorious for playing his son in a younger age group during tournaments.

****

You might need a jacket—

When you get so upset at your child's coach that you make threats against his infant son, there's no doubt that you need a jacket.

A young basketball player was such a problem for his team that the coach had no choice but to let him go. The kid's family was just as out of whack as the young player. One of them went as far as to threaten the coach's infant son.

****

You might need a jacket—

When the coach tells your child that she will have to work hard in the off-season if she wants to get more playing time the following season, and you respond by calling a meeting with the coach and the school principal in an attempt to get the coach fired, you might need a jacket.

At the end of each season, one coach would have individual meetings with each of his players to tell them what his expectations were for the summer and the next season. He told this particular player that she needed to work on many things if she was going to play the next year, because there was going to be a lot of competition for playing time. Not liking what she heard, the young lady left the meeting and went crying to her parents. Her father was immediately on the phone with the school administrators. He managed to get a sit-down with the principal and demanded that the coach be fired for what he'd supposedly done to the man's daughter. Evidently, the father did not mention to his daughter that she ought to work on her game and get better during the summer. Let's get the coach fired! That will solve all the problems.

****

You might need a jacket—

When you accompany your child's team on an out-of-town trip for a tournament and you sleep in your van instead of spending the money for a hotel room, you might need a jacket.

The particular gentleman was pretty well-to-do financially, so paying for a hotel room was no problem. He was just cheap. Not only did this thrifty parent stay in the family van instead of getting his own hotel room; when his kids left the hotel to play their games, he would go into their rooms to take a shower and get cleaned up.

****

You might need a jacket—

When your child is trying out for a high school team, and you send threatening letters to other children in an effort to discourage them from trying out for the same position, you might need a jacket.

****

You might need a jacket—

When you run out onto the soccer field to attack a child from the opposing team, you definitely need a jacket.

At a girls' soccer game between two city schools a few years back, a fight broke out between two girls from the opposing teams. Seeing her daughter involved in the fight, the mother of one of the combatants sprinted onto the field to get involved in the action.

****

You might need a jacket—

When your child decides to attend college hundreds of miles away from your hometown just to get away from you, you might need a jacket.

When a girls' basketball standout grew tired of her father's constant badgering and criticism during her high school career, she came up with her own remedy. During the college-recruiting process, she eliminated every school within driving distance of St. Louis and only looked at schools on the East and West Coasts. She wanted to get as far away from her overbearing father as she could. She ended up choosing a school in the East—a safe distance away from Daddy.

****

You might need a jacket—

When you have sexual relations with a college coach in an effort to help your son get a scholarship, you might need a jacket.

Yes, we saw Sally Field's character do this to get her son into a school in the movie Forrest Gump, but it also happened right here in St. Louis about twenty years ago. A coach was recruiting a talented basketball player and he gave the kid's mother a ride to her son's game. The mother, who loved the idea of her son getting a scholarship to this coach's school, unbuckled her seatbelt in the car and proceeded to perform a sexual act on him while he was driving.

After the game, the coach gave the mother a ride home. When they got to her place, she immediately went upstairs and called for the coach to go up to her bedroom. The coach went upstairs and walked into her room to find her completely naked and ready for action. The rest is history. By the way, the young man had his own ideas about his future education. He wound up choosing a different school.

****

You might need a jacket—

When you throw a soda at the radio-broadcast team in the press booth during your son's football game, you might need a jacket.

A couple of radio announcers used to broadcast all of Belleville Althoff's home games from Township Stadium. While we were covering an Althoff game, one of the announcers told me about what had happened when, during one broadcast, he made a critical comment about one of Althoff's players. Evidently, that player's father was at the game, listening to the broadcast on a Walkman radio while watching his son play. Miffed by the critique of his son's play, the parent took a large cup of soda and threw it at the two announcers in the press box.

****

You might need a jacket—

When you kick dirt on your own child after she is thrown out at third base during a softball game, you might need a jacket.

In a girls' softball game, the manager of the team was coaching third base when his daughter was thrown out at third base. She slid right in front of her father as she was tagged out, and the frustrated coach reacted by kicking dirt on her. For good measure, he went into the dugout, took her softball glove, and threw it over the fence. Nice, Dad!

****

You might need a jacket—

When your lawn chair is tossed by another parent because she cannot stand to be around you any longer, you might need a jacket.

Two women were sitting in their lawn chairs, watching their daughters play in a youth softball game. One of them spent the entire time complaining and yelling at the umpire. The other lady, at her wits' end, told the woman to stand up for a minute. Then she picked up the woman's lawn chair and hurled it several feet down the baseline. The first woman got the picture, moved down the line and sat down. The other woman finally got to watch the game in peace.

****

You might need a jacket—

When you curse out the college basketball coaches who call your house to recruit your child, you might need a jacket.

In the early 1990's, a young basketball player had colleges from all over the country recruiting him. However, this player's mother wasn't one who liked to have her phone lines tied up. She did not care too much about the recruiting game. Whenever a coach—many of whom were from big-time college programs—would call to talk to her son, he was greeted with a good old-fashioned cursing-out.

The conversation usually went something like this:

"Hello. This is Coach John Smith, from Big-Time University. May I speak with your son about our school and the possibility of a scholarship?"

"Hell, no, you stupid m&*%% f&%*#! My son is not here. And don't you ever call me again, you blankety-blank, bleeping bleep. Bleep you!" And she'd hang up.

I know this to be true, because when I called the young man's house in an attempt to get him to play in a post-season all-star game; I got a similar response from his mother.

****

You might need a jacket—

When you put a brown paper bag over your head every

time your kid makes an error at his Little League Baseball game, you might need a jacket.

Yes, there was a father out there who would don a paper bag each time his young son made an error on the field. That must have been good for the young lad's self-esteem!

****

You might need a jacket—

When your child begins to listen to you during a game instead of to his or her coach, you might need a jacket.

When you manage to get your child's attention during a game, and he or she begins to listen to you instead of the coach on the bench, it's time to be quiet.

****

You might need a jacket—

When you let your own mother pressure you into writing about your brother in a newspaper article, you might need a jacket.

My mother, Sandra Austin, did not like anybody criticizing her kids.

When it came to her advocating for her kids, I did not escape her wrath. While I was still covering sports, my younger brother, Richard, came along as a high school basketball and baseball standout. Sometimes that made things interesting at home. My mom got on my case, making sure I wrote about my brother in the paper. She was quick to remind me that while I was writing about everyone else's children, I had better not forget to write about her youngest child. I did not forget.

****

You might need a jacket—

When you yell out your child's pet nickname in a crowded gymnasium during a game, you might need a jacket.

Yes, it's dear Mama once again. Ever since I was little, her pet nickname for me was Yuvee (rhymes with Lovie). It was a nickname that usually stayed in the house which was the way I wanted it. My God, she called me Yuvee, for goodness' sakes! Anyway, during my senior year, I stepped to the free-throw line to shoot a free throw against our rival, McCluer. When I received the ball, the gym got real quiet for some reason. As I prepared to shoot, a loud voice rang out through the huge crowd. "Come on, Yuvee! You can do it!" The voice was unmistakable. It was my mother. I was a little embarrassed—so much that I had to step off the free-throw line to compose myself. It did not help that some of the players on the line were snickering at me, including the referee who'd handed me the ball. Thanks, Mom! I love you.

****

You might need a jacket—

When you call a reporter a fat hog at a basketball game, you might need a jacket.

The fat hog was me, and the person who leveled that verbal barb at me was the mother of a former local basketball star. She is the greatest, but she is one who's never had a problem speaking her mind. She's never had a problem with volume, either—plenty of it! In the mid-1990's, I was doing radio play-by-play for high school games on KATZ. One of the top players in a game I was broadcasting was this lady's grandson. This young man wore thick goggles, and I made the comment on the air that he looked like Steven Ercle, the nerdy star character on the hit television show Family Matters. A couple of weeks later, I walked into a gym in the city to see another game. As soon as I walked in, I heard a loud, raspy, unmistakable voice from the crowd.

"Earl Austin, I heard you on the radio calling my grandbaby Ercle. You fat hog!"

Everyone sitting near the woman got a good laugh out of that one. I admit, I started laughing myself. Only a few people walking this earth can call me a fat hog and make me smile. This dear old woman is one of those people.

****

You might need a jacket—

When you blame everyone else for your child's shortcomings (such as lack of talent, questionable grades, and bad attitude) instead of holding your child accountable, you might need a jacket.

****

You might need a jacket—

When you call a sports-radio talk show on behalf of your husband, who happens to be an All-Pro National Football

League quarterback, to refute comments made by your husband's head coach, you just might need a jacket.

The rags-to-riches story of quarterback Kurt Warner, who went from supermarket employee to Arena League sensation to Super Bowl hero with the St. Louis Rams, is well-documented in sports folklore. While Kurt became St. Louis's top sports celebrity, his wife, Brenda, made quite a name for herself as her husband's number one fan and most loyal advocate. This was never more apparent than on the morning of December 3, 2002, when Brenda decided to pick up the phone and call a sports-radio talk show to speak her mind on Kurt's behalf, in the ultimate "stand by your man" moment. Her comments caused quite a stir in the St. Louis community and made national headlines throughout the National Football League.

Co-hosts Bryan Burwell and John Maracek, of all-sports radio station KFNS, were the recipients of Brenda's surprise phone call. First, she chastised them for a lack of knowledge of a certain situation. Then she went on to contradict comments made by Rams head coach Mike Martz, basically calling him out on the radio as someone who was not telling the truth.

The scenario centered on a hand injury that Warner suffered late in the 2002 season. Being a tough guy and a true competitor, Warner insisted that his hand was fine and he was healthy, even after he'd struggled through a 10-3 loss against the Philadelphia Eagles on Sunday, November 30. After that game, Warner was told to have his right (throwing) hand X-rayed to see if there was any damage. The X-ray revealed that he had a broken bone in his hand.

Burwell had a chance to talk with Coach Martz on the Monday after the game, and Martz told Burwell that they'd told Warner to get the X-ray. The following day, on his talk

61

show, Burwell broached the subject of Warner's injury and posed the question as to whether trust between Martz and key Rams players had been shaken in regard to injuries. Brenda happened to be listening to the show. That's when she picked up the phone and the fun began. The game of he said/she said about who actually told Kurt Warner to get an X-ray on his hand turned into an ongoing soap opera.

"When our producer came in the studio and told us that Brenda was on the line, John (Maracek) just starting laughing," Burwell said. "He knew who it was, but I had no idea. I thought it was just a friend of John's named Brenda, wanting to call the show. When she started talking, that's when I realized it was that Brenda. At the time, I didn't know where this was going to go, but I knew that when we got there, it was not going to be good. Here you have the wife of the star quarterback on the line, and she basically calls his boss a liar. At first, I thought, 'Oh, boy,' but then I said to myself, 'Oh, boy! This is happening on my show'."

Here is how the ninety-second conversation went down on the radio. (From the St. Louis Post-Dispatch, Dec. 4, 2002.)

John Maracek: "Brenda?"

Brenda Warner: "Yes."

Maracek: "How are ya?"

Brenda: "I am good, but..."

Maracek: "Is your husband okay?"

Brenda: "I cannot believe how uninformed you are."

Maracek: "I know. Can you help us?"

Brenda: "Yeah, I can help you, but you know how the

media takes it."

Maracek: "Hmm."

Brenda: "So you guys are part of it."

Maracek: "We'll take notes."

Brenda: "Martz did not insist that he get an X-ray."

Maracek: "Thank you."

Brenda: "Martz had nothing to do with it."

Maracek: "Okay."

Brenda: "So his trust level has not been shaken. He had nothing to do with it. All week I told Kurt to get an X-ray. The doctors never once said that he should get an X-ray. So I don't understand how you can take that and just say that the confidence is blown."

Bryan Burwell: "Well, Mike (Martz) said yesterday that he told Kurt, 'You've got to get an X-ray.'"

Brenda: "He did not."

Maracek: "Okay."

Burwell: "Okay."

Brenda: "He did not. All week long, I said, 'Kurt, I am a nurse. You should get an X-ray.' He said, 'The doctors just think it's bruised.' So don't take, like, a little piece and make it into a whole different story. This is big enough the way it is, and so ridiculous that...don't even act like the confidence is blown. You don't even know the relationship there. So that is what frustrates me more than anything, is how the media has taken this and turned it into something that it's totally not. So I am going to trust that fans and people that care about people realize that this isn't what it is portrayed to be."

The phone line went dead. The conversation ended right there.

After the show, Burwell got a tape of the segment, took it to the Rams' facility, and played it for the public relations staff, who then took it up to Martz for his listening pleasure.

Six years later, Burwell, who is also a columnist for the Post-Dispatch, still shakes his head at the whole incident. "I don't know who was right or wrong, but what I do know is that your significant other cannot go on a radio show and start questioning the coach of the team. Once she got on the air, I knew it was going to be an absolute disaster. I think it was also the beginning of the demise of Kurt Warner in St. Louis."

****

You might need a jacket—

When you send a reporter an entire portfolio on your sibling in an effort to get him recognition for the newspaper's Athlete of the Week award, you might need a jacket.

This jacket goes to my co-worker Onye Hollman at The St. Louis American. Each week during the high school season, our sports section spotlights a top prep athlete as our Athlete of the Week. At the end of the feature, I leave the phone number and e-mail address of the paper so that people can call and nominate a young athlete for recognition. One Monday morning when I got to work, I found a five or six-page portfolio of Justin Ijei, a former prep football standout at Lafayette High, sitting on my desk. Justin is also Onye's younger brother.

The portfolio contained a one-page cover letter, a three-page letter detailing all of Justin's athletic accomplishments, his resume and a big picture of Justin. All of this was provided by Onye, who followed up by sending me an e-mail making sure I had received all the information and asking if I needed any more. It was the most detailed nomination I have ever received.

Needless to say, Justin became the Athlete of the Week. Onye works in our sales department, and she's very good at her job. Now I see why. Mission accomplished, Onye!

****

You might need a jacket—

When your child decides not to compete in sports at the collegiate level because he or she is burned out after dealing with your constant criticism throughout his or her high school career, you might need a jacket.

This one is kind of sad, because I really don't like seeing talented young people giving up on their athletic careers way before their time. But it does happen more often than people think. Sometimes a young athlete gets so fed up with the constant badgering and criticism from an overbearing parent that he feels like once his high school career is over, he's had enough.

****

You might need a jacket—

When you have your son do his weight training separately from the rest of his high school teammates, you might need a jacket.

Football is known as the ultimate team game. Everyone does his job, and the team benefits. During the off-season, the kids spend hours together in the weight room, developing team harmony while getting ready for the upcoming season. One father of a local football standout had his own ideas about teamwork. Instead of working out with his teammates, he had his son work out on his own in the weight room, with his own personal trainers.

****

You might need a jacket—

When you are a high school cheerleader and you receive a technical foul during a basketball game, you might need a jacket.

I know this scenario does not involve a parent, but I couldn't resist including it in this book. It happened several years ago during the St. Francis Borgia Thanksgiving Tournament. During a free-throw attempt, the team's cheerleaders were doing a baseline routine under the basket. The referee asked them to move back off the baseline. When he turned his back to the cheerleaders to return to the action, one of the cheerleaders pointed to the referee and said to her friend, "Who the (expletive) does he think he is?" The official heard the remark, whirled around, and gave the stunned young lady a technical foul, resulting in two free throws for the opposing team. When the head coach was told that one of his cheerleaders had cost his team two points, the look on his face was priceless.

****

You might need a jacket—

When you name your child with the nickname of your favorite college football team, you might need a jacket.

A former co-worker of mine at KASP radio was the biggest Alabama football fan I knew in St. Louis. He loved his Crimson Tide. Whenever I saw him at the station, he was quick to give me the update on how the Tide was rolling. When I saw him at a youth football game years later, he introduced me to his eight-year-old son, who was a talented young quarterback. "Earl, I want you to meet my son, Crimson." As I said, this man really loved his Alabama football. I guess the young child can consider himself lucky that his father wasn't a fan of, say, Michigan. "I want to introduce you to my son, Wolverine!"

****

You might need a jacket—

When you are banned from your child's high school games, and you react by calling the state association in an effort to make them reinstate you, you might need a jacket.

This particular woman had no problem making a spectacle of herself at her daughter's games. Whether she was yelling at her daughter, her daughter's teammates, the coach, the referees of the opposing team's players, she never failed to embarrass herself. The school's athletic director had no choice but to ban her from the gym for the rest of the season. This woman was so furious when she was barred from her daughter's basketball games for obnoxious behavior that she called the Missouri State High School Activities Association (MSHSAA) to get them to overrule the school's athletic director and overturn her ban. When they found out how the woman had behaved at her daughter's games, the MSHSAA told her that the school's athletic director was well within his rights to have her banned.

****

You might need a jacket—

When you have not had any contact with your son for virtually his entire life, yet when he becomes an All-American college athlete you show up unannounced at one of his playoff games and try to score some free tickets, you are most deserving of a jacket.

Shamefully, after being absent from his son's life for virtually his entire childhood, this man suddenly showed up at one of his son's playoff games when the boy became a college All-American and tried to get free tickets to the game. There was no shame in his game.

****

You might need a jacket—

When you risk your own personal safety while rooting for your child, you might need a jacket.

A few years back, during the IHSA Class 7A football playoffs between East St. Louis and Chicago Morgan Park, one of East Side's top defensive backs intercepted a pass and returned it seventy yards for a touchdown. It was a great athletic play, but not the most athletic play taking place at that moment. That distinction belonged to the player's mother, who was standing at the top of the bleachers with a film recorder on her shoulder when her son made his big play.

In one of the most athletic feats I've ever seen, the excited mother sprinted up and down the bleachers screaming with joy, with the recorder on her shoulder. I was really scared because I thought she might fall and injure herself, but she kept her balance and moved up and down the bleachers with speed and agility. I was more amazed at her display of athleticism than I was at her son's interception.

****

You might need a jacket—

When you try to control the process of hiring a new basketball coach at your child's school, you might need a jacket.

****

You might need a jacket—

When a college basketball coach comes to your home to recruit your son and you throw the coach out of your house, you might need a jacket.

This turned out to be one of the shortest home recruiting

visits ever. The college coach had been in the home of a prep standout for only five minutes before things came to an abrupt halt. As the coach sat down with the player and his parents, he commended the player's ability to shoot the basketball but questioned whether the boy was quick and athletic enough to play defense against the top athletes in their conference. He then told the player that he would continue to evaluate him before the college could offer him a scholarship during the late-signing period. The player's father responded by telling the coach that his son was going to sign early with a college, and if the coach was not going to offer him a scholarship, there was no need for him to waste any more time with the home visit. The father then asked the coach to leave his house.

"He did not get to stay for dinner or anything," the player said. "He missed out on my mother's blueberry pie."

Well, everything worked out for both parties. The player went on to have a Hall of Fame collegiate career at a local school, while the coach has one of the most successful programs in the region.

****

You might need a jacket—

When you fall asleep during a college recruiter's visit to your house to see your son, you might need a jacket—and some coffee.

On a coach's visit to the home of a high school basketball standout, the mother of the player fell asleep on the couch in the middle of the coach's recruiting pitch. When she woke up, the coach and the player were still talking. She reacted by saying to the coach, "What the (expletive) are you still doing here!" In case you were wondering, this is the same mother who routinely cursed out the college coaches who called her home to recruit her son.

****

You might need a jacket—

When you are so obnoxious and intrusive to a college coach on his home recruiting visit that he withdraws his scholarship offer from your relative, you might need a jacket.

A high school football standout decided to let his uncle sit in on the recruiting visits he received because the uncle was a former college football player himself and would know what questions to ask the visiting coaches. It was a nice idea, but it turned out to be a disaster. When one coach came to visit, the uncle hit the coach with every question in the book. He was downright rude and obnoxious, to the point where the coach decided to withdraw the scholarship offer from the stunned young player.

****

You might need a jacket—

When you are a high school basketball coach and you send one of your bigger players out to physically manhandle an opposing player who is messing with your son, you might need a jacket.

In the late stages of a Christmas Basketball Tournament game between a Metro East team and a team from Chatham-Glenwood, one of Glenwood's players started messing with the son of the other team's coach, who was much smaller than this player. The Glenwood player blocked one of the kid's shots and proceeded to taunt him for the next few minutes, getting a little carried away. Incensed at watching this player taunt his son, the coach decided that it was time to teach the young punk a lesson. He pointed down his bench, and up jumped a burly 260-pound behemoth who was an All-State linebacker on the school's football team. As he took his warm-up jacket off to check into the game, sportswriter Dave Wilhelm, of the Belleville-News Democrat, said, "Uh-oh, here comes Tony Twist," referring to the St. Louis Blues hockey enforcer. When the enforcer entered the game, the coach called for a play in which his son was to dribble up the court and the enforcer was to set a screen against the son's tormentor. As the coach's son got to the elbow of the free-throw line, the linebacker stepped up and delivered a bone-crunching screen on the chatty Glenwood player, knocking him flat on his back. After that, there was no more taunting.

****

You might need a jacket—

When you transfer your child to a different school because you are jealous of the attention and publicity your child's teammate is getting, you might need a jacket.

One of the great dynamics of youth sports occurs when a team has two star players. Things can get real interesting—especially between the parents of the two teammates. Each parent wants his or her child to be the star, even at the expense of the other child. I've seen many situations where the kids get along great but the parents have utter disdain and dislike for each other.

Years ago, a local high school won a state basketball championship, remaining undefeated behind the outstanding play of two stellar players. They were awesome. One became the player of the year and an all-state performer, receiving numerous accolades, while the other player did not get as much publicity. This did not sit well with his parents. They wound up transferring their child to a rival school, where their kid could be the star.

Another local school had one of the top basketball teams in the area, led, again, by a stellar pair of guards. These two kids put their school on the map in high school basketball. They were good friends, but their parents could not stand each other. It had not started out that way. Everything was harmonious at the beginning, until one of the players emerged as a top player, getting the lion's share of the publicity. This did not sit well with the parents of the other player. It was on!

Each set of parents wanted their kid to be the star, and the only thing standing in their way was the other kid. The parents would slam the other kid any chance they got, and the poor coach was caught in the middle. He had to field the parents' complaints about why he was favoring the other kid over their own child. "Why do you let that kid shoot so much?" "He won't pass my kid the ball!" "My kid should be playing point guard, because the other kid turns the ball over too much." This back-and-forth went on throughout the students' careers, and the coach most certainly got dizzy.

Both sets of parents monitored the statistics of the other family's kid and whatever publicity the kid got in the newspaper, radio or television. If they felt that their kid was getting shortchanged, the coach would get a phone call. It got to the point where, in the summer tournaments, the parents did not want to kids to even play together. The parents would find out if the other kid was going to play in a summer tournament before they made their decision if their child was going to play. When the summer coach would ask one parent if they were coming, they would ask if the other kid was going to be there. If the answer was yes, they would decline..It was pretty silly stuff, yet quite entertaining.

A few years back, a young man received All-Area recognition from the local newspaper in his sport. He was an excellent player, but he had a much more heralded teammate who was named Player of the Year. In the kid's All-Area bio, the writer mentioned the name of the more heralded teammate which sent the kid's mother into a tizzy. The mother called the writer to complain about how her kid was in his teammate's shadow all the time and how heartbreaking it was for her to see that boy's name mentioned in her son's All-Area bio. During this phone call, she became emotional to the point of tears.

Oh, boy!

****

You might need a jacket—

When you choose what high school your child is going to attend because you think you will be able to have more influence in that school's affairs than you would in another school, you might need a jacket.

****

You might need a jacket—

YOU MIGHT NEED A JACKET

When your son is a track-and-field standout, and you run alongside him while he is finishing a race, you might a jacket.

A few years back, a North County school had an athlete who was one of the state's top performers in the 800-meter run. The runner got plenty of support for his efforts from his mother—especially when he put on his finishing kick to win the race. As he came down the final straightaway, his mother was running right alongside him in the infield, screaming at the top of her lungs. It was a hoot.

However, that was quite an improvement over what she used to do. Initially, the mother would run along with her son on the inside of the track for the entire 800-meter race. That was until the coach told her she could no longer run the race with her son in such a manner.

Another mother who loved to follow her son down the final straightaway at the end of his races got a little too involved in one of the boy's races. As she sprinted along the fence, following her son, she did not see a woman who was standing in her path. The mother plowed into the unsuspecting lady and knocked her to the ground. What made the situation worse was that the woman who was knocked over was eight months pregnant.

Another enthusiastic track mother had one of the most distinctive voices ever heard at a track-and-field meet. Her sons used to run for Kirkwood High as sprinters. Whenever the sprint relay race would start, she would start screaming at the top of her lungs, "Go Kirkwooooood! Kirkwoooood!! Kirkwoood!!!" over and over again until the race concluded. You could hear her in the next county.

****

75

You might need a jacket—

When you are holding tryouts for a summer basketball team and you try to cut every player that might play the same position as your child, you might need a jacket.

A local summer basketball club holds an annual two-day tryout session to choose who is going to play on their teams for the summer. The teams are chosen by a committee of coaches, who get together at the end of the tryouts to discuss their evaluations. At one tryout held several years ago, one of the coaches on the committee had a son who was trying out for the team as a guard. As the discussion went on, it became clear that the father had a clear agenda. Whenever it became time to discuss a player who played the same position as his son, he would bad-mouth and ridicule the young man to the other coaches, hoping to convince them to cut those players and create more opportunities for his son.

****

You might need a jacket—

When you pull your child off his high school team three times in the middle of the same season without any warning, you might need a jacket.

****

You might need a jacket—

If you are constantly yelling at the referees without knowing the rules of the game, you should go to the front of the line for a jacket. Being loud is one thing, but being loud and ignorant really takes the cake.

Referees have to put up with a whole lot of static over the course of a game. They catch all kinds of grief from the fans, coaches and players of both sides. It takes a special kind of human being to put up with all that abuse and stay focused on officiating a good game. Officials will put up with a lot, but one thing they hate more than anything is the loudmouthed fan who is constantly on their case, yet has no clue about what the rules of the game are. This is probably the most common complaint I've gotten from referees.

****

You might need a jacket—

When you try to pick a fight with an entire cheering section after they make derogatory remarks about your sibling, you might need a jacket.

Those all-boy Catholic school cheering sections can be pretty relentless—at times, brutal—when it comes to taunting members of the opposing teams. One such incident occurred several years ago at the Vianney Basketball Tournament, when the host, Golden Griffins were playing against a North County opponent that featured one of the area's top players. The Vianney student section decided to turn their attention to this player, jeering and taunting him at every opportunity. It was pretty harsh stuff. Midway through the third quarter, the player's oldest sister stalked across the floor during a time-out, got in front of the student cheering section and challenged them all to fight. She was eventually restrained by her family members. The young woman was steaming mad, and she wanted a piece of anyone who was taunting her little brother. I don't know if any of those boys wanted to take her on, she was that angry!

****

You might need a jacket—

When you only cheer if your child makes a good play, you might need a jacket.

****

You might need a jacket—

When you live your life through the success of your child, you most definitely are in need of a jacket. This may be the most popular form of straitjacket behavior.

****

You might need a jacket—

When you try to chase the referees off the court at the end of a basketball game, you might need a jacket.

The scene was a high school tournament, and a school from West County was losing to a team from Jefferson County by three points in the closing seconds. The team from West County's top player dribbled up the court and stopped at the three-point line to attempt the game-tying three-point shot. He gave a fake shot and got his defender up in the air. As he went up for the shot, he was clobbered by the defender. It was an obvious foul. However, there was no whistle on the play. The game was over, and the team from Jefferson County won by three points.

But the fun was just beginning. I was sitting in the front row with another high school coach, who was there scouting the game. Sitting at the top of the bleachers was the father of the young man who'd been fouled on the last play. When we saw that there was no foul on the play, the coach and I looked at each other with the same thought: We knew the father was on his way down. "Here he comes. Let's get him!" No sooner was that said than you could hear the father's loud footsteps pounding down the bleachers. He was as red as an apple with anger. Within an instant, the father was on the court, trying to get to the referees. The referees made a mad dash off the court with the dad in hot pursuit. Luckily, the coach got to the father and led him off the court without incident.

****

You might need a jacket—

When you transfer your child from one school to another and you tell the coach of the school you're leaving by faxing him a letter, you might need a jacket. A face-to-face meeting might be more appropriate.

****

You might need a jacket—

When you make derogatory remarks about the other kids on your child's team during a game, you might need a jacket.

This can be dangerous territory for a parent. If you partake in this kind of behavior, not only do you need a jacket, you may also need some boxing gloves, because the chances are good that if you get too carried away with your criticism you might be fighting one of your fellow parents.

These situations can get real dicey.

****

You might need a jacket—

When you visit your son at his college and decide to stay in his dorm room instead of getting a hotel room, you might need a jacket.

A local basketball standout was at college during the summer session, living on campus and attending summer classes. His mother visited him for a weekend. Instead of getting a hotel room, she decided that she wanted to stay in the dorm room with her son and his roommate so she could keep track of him. It was a little crowded in the room that weekend. Being called a Mama's boy in college must have really helped this poor lad's image!

****

You might need a jacket—

When you call your child's coach on his cell phone in the middle of a game to complain about the lack of shots your child is getting, you might need a jacket.

This father was not even at the game his daughter was playing in, which was in a tournament out of town. However, he was keeping tabs on the game: His wife was at the game and would report to him by cell phone. When the wife told him that their daughter was not getting enough shots, the father decided to call the coach at halftime to complain about his daughter not getting the ball enough.

****

You might need a jacket—

When you give a school's athletic director an ultimatum that he has to fire your child's coach, and you transfer your child to another school when he refuses to do so, you might need a jacket.

A father stormed into the athletic director's office one day, demanding that the director fire his son's coach because the man did not like him. The athletic director told him that he would not fire the coach, so the dad pulled his child from the school and put him into another one.

****

You might need a jacket—

If you are out drinking and socializing with your child's coach on a routine basis, you might need a jacket.

****

You might need a jacket—

When in the middle of the play you tell your child to stop running up the basketball court so that you can take a picture of her with the ball, you might need a jacket.

Honestly, this overzealous dad was watching his daughter dribble up the court, and he popped out a camera and wanted her to stop in the middle of the action so he could take a picture. I know this is hard to believe, but it actually did happen.

****

You might need a jacket—

When you are at a basketball game, you see your child sitting on the bench, and you go and tap your child's coach on the shoulder and ask him to put your child back into the game, you might need a jacket.

It takes a lot of guts for a parent to do something like this in the middle of a game. One father I know was displeased with how his son's team was playing, as well as with the style of offense that was being employed by the coach. He took it upon himself to go down to the team bench, tap the head coach on the shoulder and tell him to change his offense. He even made a few suggestions of his own. The coach responded by telling the father to go back up to his seat and never, ever come down to his bench again. Miffed by the coach's response, the father went back up to his seat and stewed for the rest of the game.

****

You might need a jacket—

When you take your girlfriend's car to go play in a Summer League Basketball game without her permission, you might need a jacket.

Okay, this is not about a parent, but the story is so funny I had to include it in the book. Consider it a bonus. Plus, I had a close-up view of this event. The subject of this story is a standout high school basketball player from Metro East who led his team to the semi-finals of the River-City Pro-Am Summer Basketball League at Vashon High.

In the semi-finals, this player was dominating the game with his perimeter shooting and open court play. He could not miss. His team appeared well on their way to the championship game. Midway through the second half, a young woman entered the Vashon gym in a rage. She was cussing up a storm and hollering, "Where are my (expletive) car keys?!" The young woman, who was accompanied by two police officers, happened to be the girlfriend of the player who was dominating the game. Evidently, he had taken her car without permission so that he could get to the game.

The two policemen headed over to the team's bench and asked the team which one of them was the culprit. Everyone on the team quickly sold out their teammate and pointed him out to the policemen. He turned the car keys over to the cops, who gave them to the enraged young woman. She left in a huff, but not without one more parting shot. As she was leaving, she barked to her boyfriend, "All your (expletive) is in the parking lot, you (expletive, expletive)!" Visibly shaken by this turn of events, the player missed every shot and the team lost the game—and a berth in the championship game.

As everyone was leaving the gym, we noticed a bunch of clothes in the parking lot. The young lady had indeed taken all her boyfriend's clothes from their place and spread them all over the Vashon parking lot. Hell hath no fury like a woman with no car.

****

You might need a jacket—

When you throw a football at your son because he dropped a pass, you definitely deserve a jacket.

Youth football is a good breeding ground for straitjacket parents. The coaches yell and scream at the youngsters as if they're conducting National Football League training camps, and the parents can get way out of control. At one practice I witnessed, a young nine-year-old dropped a pass during a passing drill. His father got so mad at him that he picked up the football and threw it at the young lad. Using good footwork, the little guy managed to elude the ball. The father then got in his son's face and started yelling at the top of his lungs, "Do you want to play football?" The kid sheepishly nodded his head. The father responded, "Then act like it!"

****

You might need a jacket—

When you pull your child's baseball team off the field to chastise them, and you are not a coach, you might need a jacket.

At a Little League Baseball game, a frustrated parent was so upset at the play of his son's team that he stood up in the stands and yelled to them, "Get off the field, now!" The little guys sprinted off the field and toward the parent who had barked at them. The problem was that this parent was not a member of the coaching staff. He was just a fan and a parent of one of the players. The umpire turned to the coaches, who were just as stunned as he was by this turn of events. Meanwhile, the angry parent came out of the bleachers and gave his son's team a tongue-lashing before sending them back out onto the field. The kids went out and played like the St. Louis Cardinals—and won the game easily.

****

You might need a jacket—

When a school district gets a restraining order to ban you from sitting at a certain place at your son's baseball games, you might need a jacket.

Years ago, a high school in South County was so frustrated with a father who made a fool of himself by going behind the backstop at his son's baseball games that they sought and received a restraining order to have him moved from behind the backstop. He could still come and watch his son's team play, but he had to do it from the left field corner, well away from the action.

****

You might need a jacket—

When you have your lawyers get a court injunction to make sure your sons, who have been suspended, play in a big football game against their rivals, all of you might need jackets.

Several years ago, several members of a high school football team from the Metro East were caught drinking at a party and suspended for the next game, per school-district rules. However, the game was going to be against their main rival school, and a conference title was on the line. The parents of the suspended players immediately got lawyers, and eventually a judge issued an injunction to postpone the suspension so the boys could play in the big game. The incident touched off an outcry in the community that split the small town right down the middle, in what turned out to be one great big soap opera. Radio talk shows up and down the dial were flooded with emotional calls expressing strong opinions about how the situation had been handled by everyone from the players to the parents, the school administrators, the lawyers and the judge.

****

You might need a jacket—

When your own daughter bans you from attending your grandson's basketball games, you might need a jacket.

This happened to my friend Ronald Golden, who was one of the originators of the title "straitjacket parent." After attending the practice of his eight-year-old grandson, Ron went over to have a word with the coaches. On the ride home, his daughter informed him that she did not want him to attend any more of her son's games. Yes, Grandpa was being banned. What happened to bring about this turn of events? Evidently, while observing the practice Ron had heard the coaches using football terminology instead of basketball terminology, and after practice he had told the coaches that they sounded more like football coaches than basketball coaches—basically insinuating that they did not know anything about basketball. The coaches told Ron's daughter about their discussion, and she summarily banned her father from attending any more of her son's practices or games.

****

You might need a jacket—

When you position yourself behind the backstop at your son's baseball games to let him and his teammates know where the opposing team's catcher is setting up to receive the pitch, you might need a jacket.

An overzealous father was so excited about getting his son's team an edge that he sat behind the backstop to tell each batter where the catcher was setting up to receive the pitch. Naturally, a parent from the opposing team saw this going on, so he went down and confronted the father. An argument ensued, and the two men had to be restrained.

****

You might need a jacket—

When you try to get your daughter to skip practice with her college basketball team in order to come home and babysit her younger sibling, you might need a jacket.

This particular mother had a daughter who played Division I Collegiate Basketball, but she had no idea of the responsibilities that go along with that scholarship. She would routinely try to get her daughter to skip practice to come home and babysit her younger brother while the mother was out working. It took the daughter's college coach to explain to the mother that things do not work that way in Division I Athletics.

****

You might need a jacket—

When you go out on the soccer field in the middle of your child's game and give her a high-five after she has scored a goal, you might need a jacket.

One of my fellow media colleagues gets the jacket on this one. About four years ago, he was taking his oldest daughter, then six years old, to her final youth soccer game.

The little girl told her dad to hurry up because she was going to score her first goal of the season. As fate would have it, she made good on her promise and scored a late-game goal after stealing a pass from the goalie. That sent her father into action. As the happy girl made her way back to midfield for play to re-start, she was greeted by her father, who had run out on the field to give his baby girl a high-five.

Said Dad, "I just remembered what she said about scoring her first goal, so I calmly ran onto the field, gave her a high-five and ran off the field"—and into this book.

****

You might need a jacket—

When you show up at your child's sporting events dressed as if you are going to a nightclub rather than a high school basketball game, you might need a jacket.

In the middle 1990's, the mother of a high school basketball standout loved to be the center of attention at her son's games. She got the attention by showing up at games wearing the most provocative and revealing outfits she could find. This woman had the whole ensemble: short skirts, high-heeled pumps, thigh-high boots, fishnet stockings, tight sweaters and leather outfits. You name it, she had it—and then some! It was a sight to see. It made you wonder if she had taken a wrong turn on the way to the nightclub and ended up at the gym by mistake.

This mother had all heads turn when she walked into the gym. The fans, including other mothers, would ask the same question after every game: "Did you see what that woman had on tonight?" Only they used more unflattering terms.

You could just imagine how the teenage boys in the house reacted when this hot-to-trot mother hit the scene. The woman was in her forties, but she made every effort to look like she was in her twenties.

****

You might need a jacket—

When you are part of the student cheering section at your child's high school basketball games, you might need a jacket.

The stepfather of one of the area's top athletes is one of the most enthusiastic parents going today. He can be seen and heard everywhere, talking up the exploits of his talented son—and I mean everywhere. If you remember the days of Muhammad Ali and his vocal sidekick Bundini Brown, then this man is the Bundini Brown of high school sports. And he has good reason: His son has been one of the area's top all-around athletes for four years.

On this particular night in February of 2009, the boy's team was involved in a big showdown against one of the area's top powers. The student section was alive and boisterous during the entire game. Right in the middle of the student section with all the kids was the father, leading the cheers.

Another father, whose daughter attends a Metro East school, also got involved in the school spirit at his daughter's basketball games. He came to the games in a camouflage outfit, ready for action. By the end of the season, the student cheering section was also showing up in camouflage, and the father would stand with the students and help lead the cheers at all his daughter's games.

****

You might need a jacket—

When you prematurely order state championship T-shirts before your children's team begins to play in the state tournament, you might need a jacket.

In 1995, the Rosary High girls' basketball team was a talented bunch of athletes with high aspirations. Made up of freshmen and sophomores, the Rebels were winning games with ease and looked every bit the part of a state championship contender. Some of the parents of the girls seemed to think so, as well. A few of them went to a local sporting goods place and ordered some Rosary: State Champions T-shirts before the district playoffs even began. Now, that's supreme confidence—especially since in the same district as Rosary was the number one team, Incarnate Word Academy, a perennial state power.

As luck would have it, I turned up at Jennings High to watch Rosary play Rosati-Kain in the district semi-finals. I happened to be sitting with an assistant coach from Incarnate Word, who was in the sport-apparel business. He got wind of the T-shirt order and informed me of what was going on.

Well, Rosary jumped out to a lead, and it looked like the big Rosary-Incarnate showdown would be on in the district finals. One problem: Rosati-Kain made a comeback and pulled off the huge upset, as a stunned group of Rosary parents looked on in disbelief. As the buzzer went off, the Incarnate Word coach sitting with me yelled over to the Rosary parents, "Hey, you better cancel that order!" Incarnate Word went on to win the state championship.

Although they had their hearts broken on this night, there

was a happy ending for the Rosary girls. They wound up winning the state championship in 1998, and they finally got to wear those championship T-shirts.

The parent boosters of Priory High are another group that belongs in the "putting the cart before the horse" category. In the mid-1990's, the Rebels had quite a football team. They qualified for the playoffs, with a good chance of getting to the state championship. Their opponent in the sectional playoffs was Jennings, a team they had clobbered by nearly forty points earlier that season. The winner would travel south to play Ste. Genevieve in the state quarterfinals.

Well, expecting another easy victory over Jennings, the Priory boosters came to the sectional playoff game equipped with printed directions on how to get to Ste. Genevieve, and they passed the directions out to the fans before the game started. Unfortunately, the area was hit with bad weather and the game was played on a muddy field. The conditions were terrible which leveled the playing field in terms of talent. Anything could happen—and it did. The underdog Jennings team scored a shocking 8-6 upset victory over Priory, crushing their dreams of a state title. After the game, a couple of Jennings fans went over to the Priory side and asked if they could have those directions to Ste. Genevieve, since the Priory fans wouldn't be needing them.

****

You might need a jacket—

When you get kicked out of your child's basketball game and end up missing his record-setting scoring performance, you might need a jacket.

This story is centered on the father of one of the area's top high school basketball players. Early in the 2009 season, the young player put on a performance for the ages when he scored fifty-two points against a rival school in a pre-season tournament. He scored twenty-six points in the fourth quarter, including a half-court shot at the buzzer that sent the game into overtime. His father was a proud papa on this day.

However, he never got to see his son at his best. Sitting in the front row, the father protested an official's call too much and was kicked out of the gym by the referee. His son's team was trailing by sixteen points at the time. So the father had to sit in the school cafeteria, while in the gym his son put on a shooting display that will be talked about for years. People walked out of the gym talking about this great performance, and all Dad could do was nod and smile. "Yeah, I wish I could have seen it myself." Hopefully, someone recorded the game for him to see. Oh, the humanity!

****

You might need a jacket—

When you yell insults at the fans of the opposing team at your child's athletic event, you might need a jacket.

A friend of mine had a son who played high school hockey in suburban West County. On this night, they were playing a school from rural Jefferson County, and the action was getting pretty heated. As you would expect, the intensity on the ice spilled over into the stands as the opposing groups of parents started to hurl insults at each other. As my friend tells me, one of the parents from the West County School stood up and bellowed to the people from Jefferson County, "Why don't you go back to your (expletive) trailer parks, you (expletive) Hoosiers!"

In the words of television broadcast icon Dick Enberg, "Oh, my!"

****

You might need a jacket—

When you still wear your child's high school letterman's jacket fifteen years after he has graduated from high school, you might need a jacket.

This nice couple had three sons who played high school basketball at the same school. At a game this past season, I ran into the mother, and she happened to have on a letterman's jacket from that school. The jacket had belonged to her oldest son, who graduated in 1994. The woman is one of the sweetest parents I know, but that definitely qualifies her to be included in this book.

****

You might need a jacket—

When you go out in the middle of the night and manicure the pitching mound at the school where your son is scheduled to pitch the next day, you might need a jacket.

More than ten years ago, a father at a West County high school had a son who was one of the area's top pitchers and was scheduled to pitch at a rival school in the district playoffs. In an earlier meeting with the same school, the young man had had a rough outing on the mound. It seems that he had a little trouble with his footing. So, to prepare for the return meeting with the school, dear old Dad showed up at the field in the middle of the night, turned his headlights on for a little light, and did some manicure work on the mound so that his son would have better footing in the big game the next day. It must be nice to have your own personal groundskeeper in the family.

****

You might need a jacket—

When you spend an entire basketball game talking trash with a player who is playing against your child, you just might need a jacket.

One local mother is wild about her son, who happens to be one of the top high school basketball players in the country. When he is on the court, she really gets after it in the stands, from a vocal standpoint. She yells instructions to her son every minute he is on the court. Any opposing player who starts to talk trash against her son had better be prepared to suffer the wrath of Mom from the stands.

The young man rarely reacts to trash-talking, except to drop jumper after jumper on his chatty adversary. He lets his game do the talking. It is a different story with Mom, who taunts the trash-talker from the stands, giving him the business any time her son scores on him or blocks his shot. She lets him have it with every verbal barb you can think of. The woman is relentless. "Take his ball, Son! He can't dribble!" "Take him to the hole, Son! He can't guard you!" Or, after her son blocks a shot from the talker, "Get that weak stuff outta here! You ain't talking so much now, are you?"

It's bad enough that the young man is scoring thirty points on you, but it's even worse when his mother is talking smack to you and reminding you that you are being served by her son every step of the way.

****

You might need a jacket—

When you are the coach of a youth football team, and you smack a kid from the other team upside the head during the post-game handshake line, you might need a jacket.

I was watching the news on KSDK one night, and they showed a video from a game at the Chesterfield Athletic Association featuring ten-year-olds. After the game, while both teams were in the handshake line, the coach of one team shoved a kid from the other team backwards by his face mask, with a little force behind the push. The stunned kid fell back a step before regaining his balance. Obviously, the father of this kid was livid as he told his story on television. The coach claimed that the kid was doing stuff to his players during the game, but still, that's not the reaction we are looking for from adults. Anyway, the coach was reprimanded pretty harshly for his actions.

****

You might need a jacket—

When you cut loose with a loud, profanity-laced tirade at the end of your child's athletic event, you definitely need a jacket.

I was at a high school basketball game several years ago at which two rival schools were playing each other for the conference championship. It was a hotly contested affair that wound up going into double overtime. Emotions were running high as the game drew to its exciting conclusion. Well, late in regulation, with his team leading by four points and less than a minute to play, one of the top players drove to the basket. He made contact with the defensive player trying to block his shot and flipped in a great finger roll off the glass. The whistle blew and the crowd went wild at the apparent three-point play that would ice the game and deliver the school's first conference championship. The player's father, as well, started to celebrate wildly after his son's great play.

However, instead of the young man going to the line to complete the three-point play, the referee emerged from the crowd and called a delayed offensive foul on the player, waving off the basket and taking a critical basket away from the home team. The home crowd began to lustily boo the referee's call, but, in one of the great straitjacket moments of all time, the kid's father became completely unhinged. He stood up with his fist clenched, his face beet-red with anger, and started screaming, "Motherf*&&%*! Motherf*%*&%! Motherf%#*%*!!" over and over and over again, getting louder each time. Other parents sitting in the section looked on in absolute horror as the dad continued for another good three minutes before a school administrator went over to calm him down.

****

You might need a jacket—

When you try to get a reporter to change his story to write about your child after a game, you might need a jacket.

Early in my career at the St. Charles Post, I was covering a girls' softball game at a St. Charles-area high school. They had this great pitcher who pitched a no-hitter in the game I covered. Naturally, after the game I ventured over to her to get a few comments about her performance. Before I could get to her, I was intercepted by the mother of the catcher of the team. That young lady was a pretty good catcher, and her mother was on a mission to get some recognition for her daughter. She started complaining to me about how nobody was writing about her daughter and the pitcher was getting too much publicity.

Then the mother decided to take things one step further. She proceeded to take me by the hand and walk me over to her daughter so I could interview her instead of the pitcher. This lady was bold!

I played along and went with the woman to talk to her daughter. The first question I asked the young lady was how she felt about her teammate's no-hitter. I could see the smoke coming from her mother's ears after I asked that question. I'm sorry, I couldn't help it. I wanted to have a little fun with the mother, since she wanted to play the part of my editor for a moment. I gave her daughter a nice write-up, as well.

****

You might need a jacket—

When you call a local radio show trying to drum up interest for high schools to recruit your thirteen-year-old son, you might need a jacket.

I was driving around one Saturday morning and listening to "The High School Huddle," a Saturday morning high school sports show on 1380 ESPN. On this day, the hosts, Jim "J.T." Thompson and Chip Nicastro, were taking calls when this man called up talking about his thirteen-year-old son, who was some sort of Little League Baseball star. He was asking the hosts if they knew of a good high school where he could send his son to play baseball, because he threw over eighty miles per hour and had this great curveball. J.T. asked the caller what school district he lived in, and the father said it didn't matter because he wanted to move his kid into whatever district had a good baseball team. He kept going on and on about his son, to the point where J.T. lost his patience and read this delusional man the riot act about what he was doing to his son.

****

You might need a jacket—

When you jump on top of the student pile to celebrate your child's game-winning shot in a basketball game, you might need a jacket.

In the semi-finals of a local Thanksgiving basketball tournament, this gentleman's son had the ball, with six seconds left and his team trailing by two points. The talented young player dribbled up court and sunk a three-pointer at the buzzer, to give his team a one-point victory. A wild celebration ensued, with the students rushing the floor and piling on top of each other. The one person who stood out was the player's father, who rushed out on the floor with the rest of the students and jumped on top of the pile. As you might expect, Dad was a little excited.

The proud father and his wife are two of the most supportive parents I know. You can always recognize the family when you walk into the gym for a game, because you see the entire family wearing the oldest son's jerseys.

****

You might need a jacket—

When you get into a shouting match with the opposing coach during a youth basketball game, both of you might need a jacket.

Sometimes, in the heat of a youth basketball game, long-standing family friendships can take a back seat to straitjacket behavior. The coach of one of the teams in question was a local sports talk show host and radio play-by-play man. The coach of the other team was this man's close family friend and a college teammate of his wife.

On this day, the friends were on opposite sides of the court in this fourth-grade tussle. Adding a little spice to the mix was the fact their sons were going against each other. The two youngsters guarded each other for much of the game, and it started to get real physical between the two ten-year-olds. The woman was not happy with the physical play, so she stood up and barked at her coaching counterpart, "Hey! You need to tell your son to stop pushing!" Standing up for his team, the announcer replied, "You need to sit down and coach your own team!"

Ah, what's a little straitjacket behavior between close family friends?

****

You might need a jacket—

When you call your daughter at her out-of-town basketball camp while doing your radio show live on the air, you might need a jacket.

A former National Football League player has been doing talk radio for many years in St. Louis. One night, while doing his Sunday night talk show, he started talking about his oldest daughter, who was attending a basketball camp at the University of Tennessee with Hall of Fame coach Pat Summitt. He decided to call his daughter live on the air, to check up on her at the camp. Dad, let the young lady breathe!

****

You might need a jacket—

When you call local radio talk shows to defend your child because the hosts are criticizing him, you might need a jacket.

The mother of a high-profile former prep basketball player is also her son's number one fan and advocate. She's never taken kindly to anyone criticizing her son, especially during his younger days.

Years ago, while listening to a local sports talk show, she heard the host and a few callers taking shots at her son. Within minutes she called the show to defend her son and give the host a piece of her mind. This woman was never shy about calling a talk show when she felt the need to defend her son.

****

You might need a jacket—

If you are a college basketball coach, and you ban your players from using some of the equipment but allow your grade-school child to use the same equipment, you might need a jacket.

A local college basketball coach ordered a piece of basketball equipment called "the gun" for his school. "The gun" is a shooting machine that enables players to take many shots in a short time, while the machine rebounds and passes the ball back to the player. However, when this coach first got the machine, he banned his own college players from using it—but he let his sixth-grade daughter use the machine whenever she wanted. That young lady is now playing Division I Basketball.

****

You might need a jacket—

When you are coaching a youth basketball team and you pull out a knife against the opposing coach during a confrontation, you are definitely straitjacket-ready.

A few years back, two youth basketball teams were playing in a tournament, and the action was really heated. The game was getting way out of control with rough play. The opposing coaches were hot under the collar, and they started barking at each other. Their confrontation got so heated that one coach challenged the other to a fight, along with the players. He told him that they could meet outside after the game to settle the issue. The other coach responded that they didn't have to wait until the end of the game, and there was no time like the present. He then proceeded to take out a knife and flash it at the first coach.

Yikes! Luckily, cooler heads prevailed, and there was no further incident.

****

You might need a jacket—

When you get on a college basketball team's chat room and take cheap shots at a player who happens to play the same position as your relative, you might need a jacket.

I was looking at this local college basketball chat room, and there was a thread discussing a certain player and how well he was playing. Well, one poster got on the board and started ripping this player. It turned out that the poster was related to another player on the team, who happened to play the same position. In essence, he was trying to talk down his relative's competition. The other posters on the board saw through this and called him out for his petty behavior.

****

You might need a jacket—

When you try to pick a fight with a member of the team your child is playing against and you almost have a heart attack in the process, you might need a jacket.

A local head basketball coach was one of his school's all-time great players when he was a student there, and his father never missed his games. A high school coach himself, the father was a nice man, but he could also be described as a tough-as-nails man from a small town—an ornery cuss, if you will. He didn't like anyone messing with his son.

On this particular night, the son's college team was playing a conference rival on the road. One of the boy's teammates went up for a dunk and was fouled hard by a rival player.

The son got in the face of the muscular opponent to protect his fallen teammate, who had been knocked down. The player responded by pushing him away. That sent the father into action. He immediately got up from his seat and rushed down the bleachers to get a piece of the player who had pushed his son.

Despite the fact that the player was less than half his age and a whole lot bigger, Dad was ready to fight for his son. It must have been quite a sight to see this little, middle-aged man in his early fifties trying with all his might to get at this twenty-one-year-old chiseled athlete to do battle. Fortunately, he was intercepted by one of the assistant coaches on his son's team, who managed to restrain the enraged father, wrestle him to the ground and take him out into the corridor to cool off.

Said the assistant coach, "A few minutes after the incident, a woman taps me on the shoulder and tells me, 'Coach, that man you just took outside—I think he's having a heart attack.'"

The excitement and stress of the incident had got to the father so much that he started hyperventilating and experiencing heart palpitations. He was rushed to the local hospital for observation and later released with a clean bill of health.

****

You might need a jacket—

If you nearly get your son sent home from his team's road trip because of your constant complaining about his lack of playing time, you might need a jacket.

Several years ago, a local summer basketball club was competing in a national tournament. It was a team with a lot of talent, so getting quality playing time could be difficult at times. The mother of one of the team members was not at all satisfied with her son's playing time, so she decided to do something about it. She had a nice plan of attack. Instead of talking to the entire coaching staff at once, she got to each member of the staff while he was by himself, and expressed her concerns about her son's lack of playing time. One by one, she picked them off. She got to the first coach outside the gym after a game. She got to the second one in the lobby of the hotel where the team was staying. She got to the third coach in the hotel elevator. The woman was good!

The coaches did not realize what Mom was up to until they had a meeting in a hotel room. Each told a different story about how the mother had come up to him and complained about her son not playing. They decided to call the player and his mother down to the room for a meeting. The young man showed up for the meeting, but the mother refused to come.

After the mother's refusal to meet the staff, the coaches handed the player a plane ticket and told him that they were sending him back home to St. Louis, along with his mother. The stunned young man could not believe what had just happened. The coaches told him that his mother was unhappy, so they were going to send him on his way. The player protested vehemently that he was happy and didn't want to leave. He convinced the coaches that he would talk to his mother and she would not be a problem anymore. The coaches relented and let the young man stay. The mother stopped her complaining.

****

You might need a jacket—

When you build a basketball gym and weight room in your new house for your child, you might need a jacket.

A former college basketball coach's oldest son was a true gym rat, who loved to play basketball at all hours. The kid ate, slept and lived the game. When the family built their dream house in St. Charles County a few years back, the father put in an interesting addition. He installed a large gymnasium with a basketball court and a weight room, so his son could work on his game without ever leaving the house. It was a sight to see. The house was situated so that the father could walk out a door in the family room and be on a balcony from which he could look down and watch his son work out. It seemed to work pretty well. The young man had an outstanding career and became the St. Louis Player of the Year.

****

You might need a jacket—

When you change your seating location at your daughter's game several times, based on how her team is doing, you might need a jacket.

This gentleman had a daughter who was playing in a recent state basketball tournament in Columbia. At the final four, his daughter's team was playing in the state semi-finals. At the beginning of the game, the father was sitting in one of the first rows behind the team bench. By the end of the first quarter, his daughter's team was trailing, and a frustrated Dad had moved up a level to Section 200 of the Mizzou Arena in Columbia. By halftime, the team continued to trail, and Dad continued to move. At halftime, he could be seen in the tunnel of Section 300, pacing up and down the hallway. By the end of the third quarter, he was leaning on the rail in Section 300 with a look of disgust on his face. By the end of the game, which his daughter's team lost, poor Dad had relegated himself to the top of the Mizzou Arena seats, where he was all by himself with nobody in sight. The father's movements were tracked by his friends throughout the game.

****

You might need a jacket—

When you get into a fight with your child's coach in the hotel room while on the team's road trip, you might need a jacket.

This incident happened between two of my good friends. One was coaching the team, and the other had a son who was playing. On this night, the two were discussing the team in the hotel room. The man with the son started expressing some opinions that the coach did not take kindly to. Before you knew it, the two were in a heated verbal exchange. That was when one of the men picked up the television remote control and threw it at the other. Enraged, the man leaped across the room and tackled his foe, putting him into a headlock. The two men rolled around the room for a few minutes before someone finally came in, saw the fight and broke them apart.

****

You might need a jacket—

When you get into a shouting match with your kid and

then your wife at the same game, you might need a jacket.

For several years, I was the scorekeeper for my father's Little League Baseball team, the Florissant Trojans. One of the assistant coaches on the team had a son who was one of the top players. Father and son were cut from the same cloth. Both were intense competitors with quick tempers. During one game at Wiehaupt Park, the father got real upset at his twelve-year-old son for a few mistakes he made in the field. The man really read his son the riot act when he came back to the bench.

The son reacted by yelling back at his father. After a few minutes, the son took off running out of the park and into a neighboring subdivision. Seeing this from the bleachers, the man's wife went over to the bench and began yelling at her husband for how he was treating their child. A shouting match ensued between husband and wife. Meanwhile, I had to go into the subdivision to find their son and bring him back to the field. Just another day at the park. It reminded me of the scene in the movie "The Bad News Bears" when the Little League Baseball coach, portrayed by Vic Morrow, got into an altercation with his son (the pitcher) and his wife during the championship game.

****

You might need a jacket—

When you resort to cursing out your nine-year-old son to motivate him before going out to pitch an important inning, you might need a jacket.

My father, Earl Austin Sr., is the ultimate laid-back individual. He had the perfect temperament to be a Little League Baseball coach. He was patient and even-keeled at all times, but every once in a while he would cut loose with a straitjacket moment. Such an event happened back in 1986, when he was coaching my brother Richard's baseball team of nine-year-olds. On this night, we were playing a team from the Mathews-Dickey Boys Club, and it was a heated battle.

Well, the score was tied at 9-9 going into the top of the seventh inning. Richard started to trot out to the mound to pitch the last inning when he was grabbed and turned around by Earl Austin Sr., who wanted to have one final word with his youngest son before he took the mound. In no uncertain terms, my father let my brother know that he would not tolerate any base on balls in this situation. My brother took it from here.

Said Richard, "He told me, 'I don't want any s*&% in the dirt! I don't want any s$%& over people's heads! I don't want any sh%% outside! I want the ball thrown over the (bleeping) plate! You understand?'"

Richard got the message. He went out and struck out the side with only ten pitches. We scored in the bottom of the seventh inning, to win the game 10-9. Richard is now thirty-one years old, but he still remembers our father's little pep talk, word-for-word, as if it happened yesterday.

****

You might need a jacket—

When you almost fall and hurt yourself while cheering wildly for your child, you might need a jacket.

One of our close family friends has a son who is the same age as my brother, Richard. They have been friends ever since they were toddlers. The boy's father was also one of the most excitable individuals I've ever witnessed when it came to cheering for his children.

There was one night years ago when this boy and my brother were playing in an eighth-grade tournament at McCluer North High. The tournament was held on two halves of the floor, separated by a large curtain down the middle of the floor. Our vantage point for this particular game was right in front of the curtain.

Late in the game, the son made a steal and drove the length of the court to make a layup, giving us the lead. The moment the son stole the ball, the father started jumping up and screaming. When he made the layup, Dad jumped backwards, expecting to bump up against the wall. He'd forgotten that there was a curtain behind him and not a wall, and he took a nasty fall backwards into the bench of the team playing on the other side of the curtain. We thought he might have broken his back. My father and I helped him up. The man was all right, but he gave us quite a scare for a minute.

****

You might need a jacket—

When you pester a sports reporter to write an article about your son's athletic accomplishments when the boy is just three years old, you might need a jacket.

One day, several years ago, I was coming out of the post office when I ran into one of my sister's old high school friends. After exchanging greetings, she started telling me about her three-year-old son and how great an athlete he was in track and field. She told me about the races he'd won

109

and how fast his times were. I told her how cool it was to see her little son having fun, but she wasn't through. She wanted me to write a feature story on him for our sports section. She went on for nearly ten minutes, trying to persuade me to write an article on her toddler. I politely told her that may be we should wait a few years before we started writing feature stories—at least until he got out of kindergarten.

****

You might need a jacket—

If you and your son sit at opposite ends of the gymnasium at your other son's games to get a better shot at berating the referees, you both need jackets.

A former local girls' coaching legend told me that his father had a unique way of keeping the attention of the referees throughout the game. The dad would sit at one end of the gym, while his other son would sit at the other side of the gym. That way, they could have equal access to the officials when they wanted to start complaining. Said the former coach, "They never wanted to sit together because when the official went to the other side of the court, they wanted to get a shot at him."

****

You might need a jacket—

When you drive your child out of town to compete in a summer basketball program instead of playing with a team in your hometown, you might need a jacket.

A father was not satisfied with the local basketball clubs in St. Louis, so he decided to take his child to play with a club in another part of the state. He drove his child four hours each way to practice. The bad part about this scenario is that the young player rarely got to play for that team. That's a lot of gas money to spend to have your child sit on the bench.

****

You might need a jacket—

If you are officiating at a high school basketball game in which your relative is playing and you slant your calls to benefit the relative, you might need a jacket.

Years ago, at a local high school basketball tournament, an official was assigned to work a semi-final game in which his nephew was playing. The young nephew ended up shooting more free throws than the entire opposing team, as his team pulled off a big upset victory. Now, what's wrong with this picture?

****

You might need a jacket—

When you hang up the phone on your fourth-grade child because he tells you that he is going to play the sport the way he wants to and not how you want him to play, you might need a jacket.

A father was trying to teach his ten-year-old son how to shoot the basketball the correct way. However, the young child was content with his own way of shooting the ball.

This led to a little friction in the household. Finally, the next day, the father called his son from work and asked him if he was going to shoot the basketball his own way, or if he was going to listen to his father and do it the correct way. The kid responded that he was going to continue to do his own thing. Hearing this, the father told his son to "Have a nice life" and hung up on him.

****

You might need a jacket—

When you tell your intelligent child that you are going to take his school books away from him if he doesn't improve his play on the basketball court, you might need a jacket.

The father of a former basketball standout was quite frustrated with his son's lack of shooting success on the court. Not only was the young man a good player, he was a straight-A student who took plenty of honors classes. However, Dad was more concerned with his son's athletic exploits during his senior year. Finally, he told his son, "If you don't start to shoot the ball well, I'm going to take your books away from you." Now, that's a parent with his priorities in order! The young man is now a successful civil engineer in St. Louis.

****

You might need a jacket—

When you curse out a priest at a high school basketball game, you might need a jacket.

Collinsville High School has enjoyed a storied basketball

YOU MIGHT NEED A JACKET

tradition for many decades, and they have had some of the most passionate and intense fans to go along with the winning. The Kahoks had quite a little rivalry going with DeSmet in the early 1990's.

One elderly woman, who was in her seventies, was wild about her Kahoks. During an intense game against DeSmet in the championship game of the Fontbonne Tournament, one of the priests at DeSmet approached the elderly lady and asked if she could move her seat so that she would not be blocking the bleachers, where people needed to enter and exit. He wanted her to move for her own safety, because DeSmet's gym was jam-packed that night. The feisty old lady told the priest, "Why don't you go take that collar and go (expletive) yourself!"

Wow! My jaw dropped to the floor when that came out of her mouth.

A year later, the same two schools were playing in the championship game again, this time at Fontbonne College. The bitter feelings were still apparent. Many of the Collinsville fans went to sit right in the middle of the DeSmet student section which caused a big ruckus. Later in the game, a DeSmet player dove for a loose ball into the front row of the bleachers and was shaken up on the play. He did not move for a few seconds. As fate would have it, he landed in the front row of the bleachers, right in front of that same feisty old lady. Seeing the fallen player in front of her, she said, "I hope you're hurt real bad, you little (expletive)!"

****

You might need a jacket—

When you try to bribe your children with fast food and other goodies to get a good performance out of them at their games, you might need a jacket.

A local television sportscaster did not hide his desire for his daughters to perform well when they participated in youth sports. He would openly bribe them. He routinely told his girls that he would take them to McDonald's if they had a good game; if not, there would be no food. He even brought his own fast food to the game and would eat it in front of them, hoping to motivate them further.

****

You might need a jacket—

When you try to steal your child's Summer League team away from the coach after your child is replaced in the starting lineup, you might need a jacket.

Several years ago, there was a good youth basketball team that enjoyed immense success. One of the key players on that team had a dad who was pretty high up the local sports food chain for many years. When the coach replaced this dad's kid in the starting lineup before a big tournament, the father was quite unhappy, as you would expect.

However, he did not respond by complaining to the coach or lobbying to get his kid back into the starting lineup. He had something more sinister in mind; he hatched a plot to take the team away from the coach, right under his nose. The dad went behind the coach's back and met secretly with the other parents of the team, telling them that he was going to take over and start his own team. Several of the parents seemed to buy what he was selling, and it looked like he was going to get his wish, plus his revenge on the coach. That is, until he and his wife went out of the country on vacation.

While the father was away, the coach talked to some of the parents who were planning to leave and convinced them to stay. When the father returned from his vacation, he realized that everyone had changed their minds and nobody was going to join him. That put him and his son in a precarious position. The coach then paid the man a visit. He told him that despite his attempt to steal the team, his son could still play on the team. However, the father and his wife would not be allowed to attend any more practices or games. That was the deal. The father ended up taking his kid off the team.

****

You might need a jacket—

When you try to rush your injured child back into a game after she's been hit in the head by a softball, you might need a jacket.

At a local softball tournament, a fourteen-year-old girl playing third base for her team was hit in the face by a screaming line drive off the bat of an opposing player. The ball hit her squarely under her eye, knocking her unconscious for several minutes. When she came to, she was taken to the dugout, where she had an icepack applied to the eye. An inning later, the young lady went back to her position at third base. The umpire immediately came from behind the plate and said there was no way he would let her play anymore. Showing good judgment, the umpire told the coach that the girl could not play until she was checked out at the hospital. The coach seemed to understand, but the young lady's mother did not. She came out of the stands in a hostile mood, cursing and screaming at the umpire for denying her child a chance to return to the game.

****

You might need a jacket—

When your obnoxious behavior at your brother's basketball game becomes so bad that you end up being tasered by the police, you might need a jacket.

A few years ago, two men were watching their younger brother play in a freshman basketball, and they were letting the officials have it really badly throughout the game. Having heard enough, one official stopped the game and ordered the two gentlemen out of the gymnasium. They refused to leave the building. A policeman was called to the gym. He tried to get the two men to leave, but they refused. In fact, their behavior became even more hostile. That's when the police officer took out his taser gun and took both men down. And remember, this was a just a freshman basketball game!

****

You might need a jacket—

When you go down to the sidelines and give your son a back rub while his football game is still going on, you might need a jacket.

This scene featured the mother of one of the area's top high school football players. During a game, the player was shaken up and had to leave the game for a short period of time. The game was still going on, while the player sat on the sidelines getting treated. That is when the player's mother came out of the stands and down to the sidelines where her son was sitting and proceeded to give him a back rub.

****

You might need a jacket—

When you are a coach and you promote your son for post-season honors, trashing your other players who are up for the same honors, you might need a jacket.

A basketball coach was asked to provide information on two of his players for the post-season All-Conference team. One player was the coach's son, while the other player was the team's top scorer of the season. Naturally, one would think the coach would have good things to say about both his top players. Naturally, one would be quite wrong. After he gave a glowing description of his son's achievements, he proceeded to criticize and ridicule the accomplishments of his other player, thus giving his son a better chance to win the post-season honors.

****

You might need a jacket—

When you miss several of your children's milestone moments in sports because you have to be at your Friday night hangout, you might need a jacket.

Once again, we feature Lou Potsou, the originator of the

117

term "straitjacket parent." Lou has one weekly routine that runs like clockwork. Every Friday night, he and his wife spend the evening at his favorite nightclub, Mihalis Chop House which features his favorite live singer, the legendary Gene Lynn and Co. They are good, so I don't blame him for that. Lou never misses a Friday night outing at Mihalis for anything, not even for his kids.

Lou's youngest son, Manoli, is a local high school basketball official who is on the rise. Last year, Manoli received his first assignment to work the final four of the state tournament. His first game was a semi-final game on a Friday night. He was looking forward to his dad being there, but no dice. Lou was hanging out at his favorite nightspot. A year later, Lou's oldest son, Mike, who is a high school coach at Whitfield High, had a team that advanced to the district championship game for the first time. This game was on a Friday night. You know that Dad would be there to see his son coach his first district championship game, right? Nope! While the son was winning his first district title, Lou was at his favorite nightspot, tapping his toes to Gene Lynn. Two weeks later, Whitfield advanced to the state semi-finals which were to be played on a Friday night at the University of Missouri, two hours away from home. This time, Lou was on hand to see his son's team win, to advance to the state championship game. But after the game he was back on the highway for the two-hour drive home, to get to Mihalis for the evening's festivities.

****

You might need a jacket—

When you pester your husband with unimportant questions while he is trying to watch his son's team play in a state playoff game, you might need a jacket.

My friend Lou Potsou's wife, Stacy, has a variety of interests. However, sports are really not among them. Stacy always went to see her sons Michael and Manoli play during high school, but she was there to support her children. She never really followed the game.

This was quite apparent during the 1998 season, when Stacy and Lou attended the semi-finals of the Class 5A football playoffs between Pattonville and Parkway Central. Their youngest son, Manoli, was the quarterback at Pattonville. If Pattonville won the game, they would go on to play for the state championship. Lou was watching the game with great intensity, while Stacy was just there enjoying the atmosphere. However, Lou was fit to be tied as Pattonville lost the game 26-0. With each moment, he got more upset at what was happening on the field.

Meanwhile, Stacy was having a good time peppering Lou with all kinds of questions that had nothing to do with the game. "Lou, did you call the plumber this morning to come look at the kitchen sink?" "Lou, did you go to the grocery store?" Lou was already upset as he watched his son's team lose in the state playoffs, but his anger grew even more intense with each of Stacy's probing questions that had nothing to do with the game. The more Lou tried to concentrate on what was going on in the game, the more Stacy hit him with questions about yard work and household chores, simply oblivious to her husband's growing frustrations.

Watching Lou's facial expressions was priceless.

****

You might need a jacket—

When you are a basketball official attending your child's game, and you get yourself kicked out of the gym by a fellow official, you might need a jacket.

A local basketball official has a son who plays high school basketball. While at one of his son's games, the official was really giving the referee a hard time. There was no such thing as professional courtesy here; the man was relentless in his criticism, questioning the referee's ability to move up and down the floor. Finally, the referee went up to the father and ejected him from the building. The father nearly got himself suspended by the state association for his actions.

****

You might need a jacket—

When you go into the locker room of your child's team at halftime, you might need a jacket.

A father was watching his son's basketball team play for its first district championship. The game was close, and at halftime his son's team was leading. This had the father excited—so excited that he decided to follow the team into the locker room so he could say a few words of his own. He talked to a couple of the players, giving them instructions, before the coaches asked him to leave the locker room.

****

You might need a jacket—

When you send text messages to all your buddies about the birth of your first son, and you include all his future sports accomplishments in the text, you might need a jacket.

This man was obsessed with the idea of his infant son becoming an athlete. On the day his son was born, the father sent out a text message to all his friends to let them know the good news. He told them the kid's name, his weight and length; then he went on to write that the kid ran a four point five in the forty-yard dash and he had a great jump shot, fastball and curveball.

Said one of his friends, who showed me the text, "This is not a joke. This man is serious. He is a psycho!"

****

You might need a jacket—

If you are the wife of a college football head coach, and you come down to the sidelines to berate his players while they are being blown out of a game, you might need a jacket.

This scene happened several years ago at a college football game, when the state university was getting clobbered in their last game by a powerful conference opponent. The coach of the team was on the hot seat and in danger of losing his job, as this was the last game of the season. With his team hopelessly behind in the fourth quarter, the frustration level of the coach's wife went past its breaking point. In the final minutes of the team's 66-0 loss, she headed down to the front row, leaned over the bleachers and started letting the players have it. She called them a bunch of quitters and worked them over pretty good, verbally. One year later, after another dismal season, the coach was fired.

****

121

You might need a jacket—

When you walk onto the basketball court in the middle of a game to lecture the referees, you might need a jacket.

Several years ago, two rival schools were playing a hotly contested basketball game. The game was very physical, and both sides were quite frustrated with the sloppy officiating. One of the players went diving into the opposing team's bench for a loose ball and ended up plowing into the assistant coach, knocking him out cold. The game was delayed for the next few minutes. While there was a stoppage in play, the mother of one of the players came down from the stands, stepped over the fallen coach and made her way onto the court to get in the referee's face. Wagging her finger at him, she lectured the official on how he had lost control of the game.

****

You might need a jacket—

When you are so worried about your son's lack of growth that you invest in an apparatus that you think will help him grow taller, you might need a jacket.

One of my friends had a son who was a good basketball player, but the father was worried about the boy's lack of height. The young man was four- foot-eight inches tall as an eighth-grader and barely five feet tall as a high school freshman. While sitting at lunch one day, the father heard an athletic trainer telling this story about a professional basketball player who'd helped his growth by hanging upside down on an apparatus to stretch his ligaments. This discussion piqued the father's interest. He was so interested that he wound up spending $500 for one of these contraptions. His son spent much of his last year of junior high school and first year of high school hanging upside down.

"I don't think it really worked, because I only grew to be five-foot ten inches," said the boy. "Unless I was supposed to be five-eight or five-nine."

****

You might need a jacket—

When you are kicked out of your child's athletic event and dragged from the gymnasium kicking and screaming, like a child, you definitely need a jacket.

Several years ago, I was at a high school basketball game when the father of one of the players was so intense in his complaints about the officiating that he was ejected from the game. I know, that's common; but this father was not ready to leave. He continued to argue and go crazy even after he got the heave-ho from the officials.

In the end, the father had to be physically removed from the gym. It took four people to do it: two administrators, a security guard and a police officer. They held the man by his ankles and arms while he continued to scream and yell at the top of his lungs. It looked like a scene right out of the movie One Flew Over the Cuckoo's Nest.

****

You might need a jacket—

When you take your child's basketball uniform off and throw it in the coach's face after a game, you must have a jacket.

At a springtime basketball tournament, a father was less than satisfied with the playing time his son received. He decided to go down to the bench and discuss this issue with the head coach. It turned into a heated argument. The player's mother decided to join the fray. Neither parent was satisfied with what they were hearing from the coach. The mother told the kid to take off his uniform, and as she informed the coach that she was taking her son off the team, she proceeded to throw the uniform in the coach's face. And that, folks, is that!

****

You might need a jacket—

When you brag about your son's exploits on the baseball field, and you have no idea what position he plays or what he does, you might need a jacket.

As I was sitting at my desk, working on a story, one of my co-workers at The St. Louis American came up to me and announced, "Earl, you better watch out for my son's high school baseball team." I always like hearing about the children of my co-workers, so I started asking her about her son. She told me about how they were winning all their games. Then I asked her what position her son played. She responded, "Now, why would you ask me that?" I said, jokingly, "Well, it's your son, and you go to all the games." She said, "Well, he plays somewhere around second base. I don't know." I asked her if he played second base or shortstop. "Does he play on the right side of the base or the left side of the base?" "I don't know, he's just out there," was her response.

Memo: When you are going to talk about the exploits of your child, it might be a good idea to know a little about what the child does.

****

You might need a jacket—

When you get so nervous at your son's football games that you wet your pants every time he takes the field to kick a field goal, you might need a jacket.

I could not believe it when I heard this one. A local high school football and track coach told me a story about his own playing days. His mother was always nervous at his games, but she took it to another level. He told me that she would wet her pants every time he kicked a field goal. She would get that excited! I was in disbelief, so the coach told me to call his brother, who confirmed the story.

"Oh, yeah, she used to wet her pants all the time," he said. "I was sitting right there, watching her do it. She would get that nervous."

****

You might need a jacket—

When you communicate to your child by sign language at his athletic events, despite the fact that he is not hearing-impaired, you might need a jacket.

While most parents attract their children's attention at their games by yelling, one mother had a unique way of getting her son's attention without creating too much of a stir. She was a certified sign-language professional, and she taught her eight-year-old son how to understand sign language. (For the record, the young child was not hearing-impaired.) The mother told me that whenever her son would make a mistake in one of his games, she would get his attention by sending him instructions via sign language. I thought this was different and quite original. However, it got to the point where the child was always looking at his mother for her signal. That's when it got into straitjacket territory.

****

You might need a jacket—

If you throw a baseball bat at your son during practice, you are in dire need of a jacket.

My brother-in-law told me this story about when he was playing Little League Baseball as a nine-year-old. During one practice, one of his teammates dropped the ball when trying to turn a double play. The boy's father was the assistant coach of the team, and when he saw his son drop the ball, he lost it. He grabbed a bat and hurled it toward second base, right at his son. The quick-thinking son sidestepped the bat, but the angry father was not done yet. He ordered his son to take a few laps around the ballpark.

****

You might need a jacket—

If you pull out a knife during your child's basketball game because you think she was fouled too hard, you must have a jacket.

YOU MIGHT NEED A JACKET

A woman was watching her daughter play in a high school basketball game. Her daughter was heading down court on a fast break. As she went for the breakaway layup, she was knocked down by a defensive player trying to block the shot. Both girls hit the floor hard and landed in a heap. Seeing her daughter get roughed up on the play, the mother could not control her anger. She thought the other girl had tried to hurt her daughter on purpose, and she was determined to extract a little revenge. To the utter amazement of those sitting around her, she stood up in the bleachers and pulled a knife from her purse. Several other parents managed to talk the out-of-control mother back into her seat before she was able to rush the court and confront the girl who had fouled her daughter.

****

You might need a jacket—

When you sit alone in the corner of the gymnasium at your child's basketball games and talk to yourself through the entire game, you just might need a jacket.

This father was in his own little world at his daughter's high school basketball games. He would sit all alone in the corner of the gym and just talk to himself. Whether he was complaining about the officiating, critiquing his daughter's play or complaining about the coach, he would never address anyone. He talked constantly, the whole time, to nobody in particular. This was a little unnerving to watch at first, but he never meant any harm.

****

You might need a jacket—

When you are a coach, and after a game you get into your vehicle and proceed to chase the school bus carrying the players from the opposing team down the highway, you are in need of a jacket.

This story does not involve a parent, but a baseball coach at a school in St. Charles County. His baseball team had just finished playing a freshman game against a visiting school from North County. After the game, the team from North County headed back down the highway. While on Highway 40, the driver noticed a van speeding up right behind them with the driver frantically flashing his lights for the bus driver to stop. This was all happening in rush-hour traffic. The speeding driver happened to be the coach from the St. Charles County team. He forced the bus driver to pull over to the side of the interstate. The coach then got on the bus and accused the North County players of stealing money from the locker rooms. Naturally, the parents of the North County kids were outraged. First, they were furious that the coach would engage in a high-speed chase and pull their children's bus over during rush hour; then, that he would accuse them of stealing. They let their feelings be known on the evening news that night. The money issue was eventually dropped, and the coach sent a letter of apology to the school.

****

You might need a jacket—

When you drive hundreds of miles just so you can confront your child's college basketball coach about the lack of playing time he gives your son, it's time for you to have a jacket.

This particular woman had a son who was playing college basketball in the state of North Carolina. He was one of the area's top players. When his playing time started to dwindle, the mother was unhappy, so she decided to find out why her son was not playing. She got into her car and drove hundreds of miles to North Carolina for a personal meeting with the coach. She stormed into the head coach's office and slammed her fist on his desk, demanding to know why her son was not playing more. As a result, the young man's playing time dwindled even more. Eventually, he was transferred to another school.

****

You might need a jacket—

If you are constantly yelling during your child's game, to the point where you just irritate everyone who is sitting around you, we have a jacket for you.

This is not about one specific parent, because it is something that happens all the time at youth sporting events. There is always that one loudmouthed, leather-lungs relative whose voice can be heard through the entire game. He is just hollering to hear himself, but unfortunately, everyone in the building can hear him, too. When he starts, people look up and think it's kind of cute. Some even chuckle. However, as he continues to drone on at a high-decibel level, people lose patience. They roll their eyes and throw their hands in the air, but it doesn't matter. He just continues with his loud and outrageous blather. Finally, somebody musters enough gumption to take the buffoon on and scream, "Will you please shut the (expletive) up!"

****

You might need a jacket—

When you sprint across the basketball court in the middle of a game to tend to your injured child, who wasn't seriously injured in the first place, you might need a jacket.

A woman was watching her son play in a Summer League tournament in St. Charles County. It would not be a stretch to say that this lady was a little overprotective of her talented young son. This was quite apparent during one game, when the young man collided with another player and momentarily doubled over in pain. A former track and field standout in high school, the mother put her speed to good use. Without hesitation, she sprinted across the floor to see what had happened to her baby. It turned out that he had a little scratch on his index finger. He turned out to be a great high school player, while his dear mother sprinted her way into a jacket.

****

You might need a jacket—

When you come onto the basketball court in the middle of a game and hit the referee on the head with your umbrella, you might need a jacket.

This story goes back to 1970, when two Public High League teams met in a big showdown. One of the referees called a foul on a player, and a woman who was a relative of that player was quite unhappy with the official's call. She came out of the bleachers and onto the court, heading straight for the referee. Then, without saying a word, she took her umbrella and whacked him on top of the head.

"I couldn't believe it," said one of the players, who

remembered the incident with great clarity. "The woman just walked up to the referee and popped him! People were rolling in the stands."

The young lady was promptly escorted from the building.

****

You might need a jacket—

When you go against your child's wishes in choosing what college he attends, you ought to have a jacket.

A local basketball standout and his mother were constantly at odds over what college he should attend. He had his pick of several top programs, and his heart was set on attending a certain national power, but his mother wanted him to attend the state school. It caused quite a bit of friction in the household during the recruiting process. There was one incident when the mother and son were driving on the highway, and the son was going on and on about how great the program he wanted to attend was. He was excited about the prospect of going to that school, but evidently the mother had heard enough. She pulled over to the side of the highway, turned off the engine and said, "Son, I don't want to hear any more about that school. You're going to the state school, and I don't want to hear anymore about it!"

The young man signed with the state school.

This scenario was also played out on the national level a few years back, when a star girls' basketball player and her father were at odds over where she was going to attend college. She was being recruited by the top-shelf programs around the country, and she had her heart set on playing for a perennial power with several national championships and a Hall of Fame coach.

However, the father had his sights set on another national powerhouse with a stellar academic reputation. Education was important to him. The young lady wound up following her heart and committing to the school of her choice. This did not sit well with her father. Feeling spurned, he refused to sign the letter of intent. He hung up the phone on his daughter's future coach when she called the girl to get her commitment. As if that wasn't enough, the father decided to boycott his daughter's college games. He vowed never to attend any games at that school. Finally, midway through her senior year, the father relented and started to attend his little girl's games.

****

You might need a jacket—

When you criticize your children's coach so much that he decides to leave the bench to go into the stands and challenge you to take over his team, you might need a jacket.

One gentleman was coaching a fifth-grade boys' basketball team, and his team's parents were really letting him have it from the bleachers. They were relentless in their criticism of the young man. "You can't coach!" "Put my son in the game!" "You don't know what you're doing!!" You know the usual straitjacket parent stuff. At halftime, one of the mothers went over to the bench to give him a little extra verbal abuse. With that, the coach decided that he had heard enough. He interrupted the mother in mid-curse and told her that if she thought she could do a better job, she should be the coach.

The coach then left the bench and went over to the bleachers to take a seat. As he walked, he yelled to the other loudmouthed parents, giving them the same invitation to go and coach the team themselves. It was "put up or shut up" time. Not surprisingly, not one parent moved from his or her seat to take the coach up on his challenge. Everyone sat quietly for a few minutes, waiting to see how the situation would unfold. After seeing his game delayed for several minutes, the referee went over to the coach and told him that he'd made his point and now it was time to go back and coach his team.

After that game, the coach had no more problems with critical parents.

****

You might need a jacket—

If you carry articles about your children around in your wallet, you might need a jacket.

This is beginning to become a common practice with straitjacket parents. It is especially the case when their children are off to out-of-state colleges, where it's harder to keep track of them in person. Instead, the parents rely on newspaper clippings. There were several times this year when I asked a parent how his son or daughter was doing in college. The parent would respond by reaching into his pocket and pulling out a newspaper clipping that was neatly folded in his wallet. After reading the clipping, I would hand it back, but some parents would say, "Oh, you can keep that one." Wow! How many copies of those articles do you have?

****

You might need a jacket—

When you go around the neighborhood stealing newspapers off people's front lawns because your child's picture is in the paper that day—or worse, when you get your child to swipe the paper while you stay in the car—you might need a jacket.

During my junior year in high school, I got my picture in the North County Journal, playing basketball for McCluer North. It was a picture of me in a jump ball with a kid from Ritenour. It was the first time that I'd ever had my picture in the paper while playing basketball.

Needless to say, my mother was excited to see it. That night, when she picked me up from practice, we turned into our subdivision and seemed to be headed toward our house. But instead of turning onto our street, my mother took a detour to another part of the subdivision.

I asked her what she was doing, and she told me to be quiet and follow her directions. She slowly pulled in front of a house and told me to get out of the car and take the newspaper off the front lawn. I said, "Mom, we can't steal their newspaper! That's against the law." She responded, "Shut up and do what I tell you." Like a spy in the television show "Mission Impossible," I ran into the front yard, took a look around to see if anyone was watching, then grabbed the newspaper and made a mad dash back to our car under the cover of darkness. To add spice to the plot, my mother included my twelve-year-old sister, Courtney, on this escapade. We went all around the neighborhood that night, stealing newspapers. We must have come away with two dozen papers, which my mother sent to friends and relatives all over the country. On this particular night in 1982, people living in the Wedgewood subdivision had no North County news.

YOU MIGHT NEED A JACKET

****

You might need a jacket—

When you fraudulently present yourself as a school superintendent and a police officer in order to keep your child out of trouble that he has created for himself, you might need a jacket.

This story comes from one of my buddies on the Illinois side who is pretty well up-to-date on things. It began when a police officer found two high school athletes asleep in a local city park at the midnight hour. They had been drinking and they were sleeping it off in the park. The following Monday morning, the kids' actions were reported to their school. The parents of the first kid readily accepted whatever punishment that would come their way. The father of the second kid, however, was in no such mood.

The local newspaper had gotten wind of the story and was prepared to run a story on the two athletes, with their names and everything. In an effort to get ahead of the game, the kid's straitjacket father called the newspaper and identified himself as the school superintendent. He informed the paper that his son had been wrongly identified and it was actually another student who had been found in the park. He took his son's yearbook, randomly picked out the name of another student and gave that name to the newspaper.

The newspaper then went ahead and ran the story without using the kids' names. However, the paper's online blog indicated that the first athlete had been suspended from school and all athletic activities for fifteen days, that the other student was not an athlete, and that the school superintendent had verified this information. When the story broke the following day, including the information

135

that both the suspended boys were indeed athletes, it became apparent that the father had indulged in some shenanigans to keep his son's name out of the headlines. He was called into the school office to explain his actions, and the parents of the student he had picked out of the yearbook filed a lawsuit against the despicable dad.

How crazy is that? But wait, there's more. This straitjacket father called another newspaper in the area, only this time he identified himself as the chief of police. He was trying to get the newspaper to print the yearbook photo of the kid he'd picked out at random and identify him as the other kid in the park. For his efforts, the father was arrested for impersonating a police officer.

All I can say is, wow!

****

You might need a jacket—

When you maneuver yourself onto the coaching staff of your child's high school team in order to be in charge of the statistics book so that you can inflate your child's statistics, you might need a jacket.

The assistant coach at a local high school had the duty of keeping the scorebook for the team which had one of the top hitters in the area. After the game, he would call in the game's stats to the local statistics organization, and the box scores would be printed in the newspaper the following day. After a few weeks, the assistant coach noticed that the stats he called in for one particular player were different from the stats that would appear in newspaper the following day. The coach would call in numbers for the player—such as two-for-four from the plate, two singles and two runs batted in—but in the paper the next day, that player's stats in the box score would read three-for-four, two doubles and three runs batted in. How was this happening?

It became a constant pattern, so the assistant coach called the stats place to see what the issue was. The culprit turned out to be the kid's father. Evidently, the father would call the statistics place about an hour after the assistant coach had called his official stats in, and he would change his son's line in the box score. In some cases, he was taking away extra base hits from other players and giving them to his own son. Of course, the young man's batting average was inflated considerably. The assistant coach solved the problem by coming up with a password that he'd use when he called in his stats, so the father could not get his phony stats in. The player's father was never confronted, but he was upset when he saw his son's batting average in the newspaper decrease to a more realistic number. The dad went so far as to offer his services to the assistant coach, to help him in his scorekeeping efforts. This offer was refused. The father lay low for the rest of the season.

The following year, the head coach told the assistant coach that he wanted him to take a more active role in the day-to-day operations of the team and he didn't have to keep the scorebook anymore. He also informed the assistant coach that the father of the top hitter had generously offered to take over the keeping of the scorebook for his son's senior year. The man had resurfaced! Yes, this was a man with a plan. With dad keeping the scorebook, his son went on to lead the area in hitting, breaking three school records in the process.

In the words of Arsenio Hall, it's a thing that made you go, "Hmmm!"

EARL AUSTIN, JR.

****

You might need a jacket—

When you sit in the same exact seat in the arena for two different seasons, nine years apart, to watch your siblings play in the state championship game, you might need a jacket.

Yeah, this is me. Since this is the last entry in the book, it's only fitting that I tell on myself again. I'm a little superstitious when it comes to following my family's sports endeavors. In 1986, when my sister Courtney's McCluer North team won the state championship, our family sat in the corner section of the Hearnes Center in Columbia with our relatives.

Fast forward to 1995, nine years later. My brother, Richard, was playing for Cardinal Ritter for the state championship, at the Hearnes Center. I made a point to get to the arena early because I wanted to sit in the same exact seat that I had when Courtney's team won the state title. I accomplished my mission, got my favorite seat and watched my brother's team win the state title, as well.

Of course, winning the state titles had nothing to do with the talent on my siblings' teams—it all had to do with me getting the same seat for both championship games.

That's my story, and I'm sticking to it.

FINAL THOUGHTS

I hope everyone has enjoyed a look inside the world of wacky sports parents. As adults, most of us walk a fine line between being a supportive mentor and a certifiable straitjacket parent. One moment, a parent is loving and caring, the biggest cheerleader for his or her child. The next instant, that same person can become a fanatical, obsessive lunatic who loses control at a moment's notice. It really does not take much for a human being to make that leap into the dark side.

I think, as adults, we must all remember that it is about our children and not us. We must put our children first at all times. When people lose control, they think they are acting in the best interests of their kids, but they are doing the exact opposite. When a young child sees his or her parent going crazy at a game for trivial reasons, it puts the child in a terrible position. The child feels sad, embarrassed and ashamed, and there is no reason for him to feel that way. Young children should be out there on the playing fields having fun with their friends. They should not have to go to their games wondering if their parents are going to get into a fight or be led away in handcuffs. When the actions of a parent begin to overshadow what the child is doing, it's time to take a step back and remember what is really important. Don't lose sight of the young person out there!

Throughout my life, I had a great role model in my father, Earl Austin Sr. He had the perfect temperament when following my athletic career and those of my two siblings. All three of us enjoyed successful careers in sports, and he played a huge role in our development as athletes, as did my mother. He was supportive, yet he could be critical, but he was never overbearing or abusive. My father walked that fine line with great ease because he understood what youth sports was all about. He was always positive with young people, and he had a steady hand when things weren't going well.

I really tested his patience when I was in junior high school. My father's first love has always been baseball, but I preferred to play basketball, like my uncles. I played some baseball, but my heart was always with basketball. One summer, my father bought me a brand new baseball glove. A few weeks later, after playing catch, a group of us went over to play basketball at the neighborhood courts. We always stayed at "the courts" until late at night. One night, I came home from the hoops and my father asked me, "Where's your baseball glove?" Uh-oh! I'd left my baseball glove at the basketball court. My father was livid, and understandably so. He'd spent good money for that baseball glove, and I was so cavalier as to leave it at the basketball court.

He was very mad, and I think he was also a little heartbroken. In a way, by leaving that baseball glove at the basketball court, his first-born son was telling him that basketball was first in his life and baseball would not be in the mix. My father could have really lost his temper and forced me to play baseball, going overboard into straitjacket territory. Instead, he understood which sport was close to my heart and supported all my basketball endeavors with everything he had.

My father's patience was rewarded several years later when my brother, Richard, came along. He loved baseball from day one, and the two of them have enjoyed a wonderful father-son relationship, partly through baseball. When, years ago, we went to see Richard play in his first professional baseball game, Richard came out of the locker room with a baseball encased in glass. It was the game ball from his first base hit. Richard presented it to my father after the game. The moment was priceless.

As I work with my three young nephews in their athletic endeavors, I have tried to take the same patient and even-tempered approach that my father had with us. Sometimes it is not easy, because I can be a little impatient at times and I want so much for my nephews to benefit from the lessons I have learned through my life. Sometimes I raise my voice, but then I calm down, because I know that's not how my father would have handled the situation.

In closing, I would say this to all adults who have loved ones involved in youth sports: Enjoy the success of your children. Also, enjoy the process. Do not let yourself get so wrapped up in your child's athletic endeavors that you end up missing the maturation of a wonderful little athlete before your very eyes.

Take care, everyone.

If you have any straitjacket parent stories that you would like to share, feel free to contact Earl Austin Jr. at eaustin@stlamerican.com or judylbh@aol.com.

Other books by Earl Austin Jr.

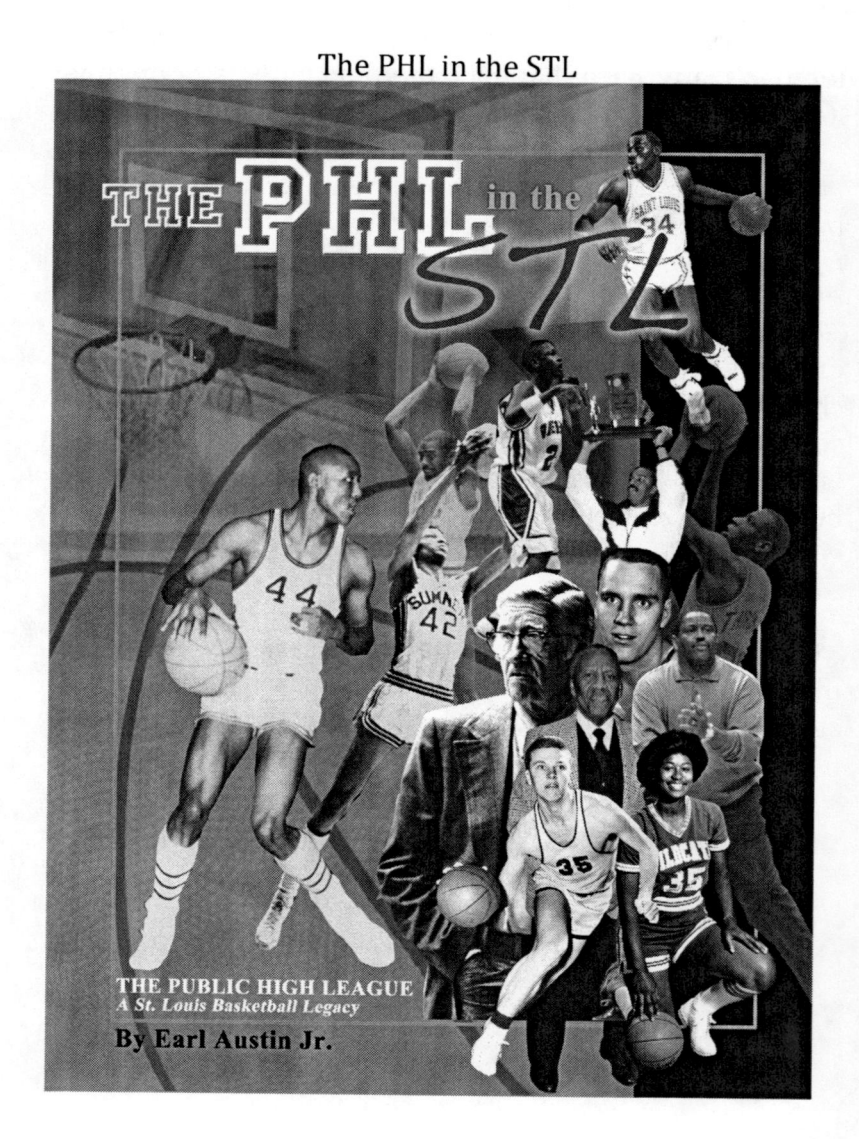

The PHL in the STL